THE ARTS
AND THEIR MISSION

THE ARTS AND THEIR MISSION

RUDOLF STEINER

ANTHROPOSOPHIC PRESS

The lectures included in this volume were given in Dornach, Switzerland, May 27-June 9, 1923, and in Oslo, Norway, May 18 and 20, 1923. The original edition bears the title, *Das Künstlerisch in seiner Weltmission* (Volume 276 in the Bibliographic Survey, 1961). Translated from the German by Lisa D. Monges and Virginia Moore, Ph.D.

ISBN 978-0-88010-154-7

Cover graphic form based
on a sketch by Rudolf Steiner.
Drawn by Emil Schweigler.

Title lettering by Peter Stebbing.

CONTENTS

INTRODUCTION

THE burden of the eight lectures here translated into English is the ineluctable connection between art and the spiritual world; and to see this central idea in context we must glance back over the history of aesthetics.

The Far East has always taken it for granted that the roots of art lie in the spiritual world. Ancient treatises describe it as expression informed by divine beauty: the Chinese *shên,* the Indian *rasa,* meaning essence, tincture, flavor, overtone of meaning, "what flashes in the lightning." The Oriental technique of vision serves this theory, and Oriental practice bears it out. The art critic Coomaraswamy, late curator of Far Eastern art at the Boston Museum, puts it this way: "Heaven and Earth are united in an analogy."

Western culture started with a similar outlook. Plato held that pure art (not mere representation) is allied with the supreme, therefore of intrinsic worth; and Plotinus developed further this doctrine of universal beauty. Christian artists during the first thirteen centuries agreed; and the Schoolmen, including Aquinas, gave it philosophical support. Meister Eckhart sums up their attitude: "In making a work of art the very inmost self of a man comes into outwardness"; that is, man's highest principle, the "image and likeness of God." Thus the perfection of art—its wholeness, harmony, lucidity—"prepares all creatures to return to God."

But the Renaissance shifted emphasis. As thinking became more and more man-centered instead of God-centered, spiritual awareness withered and died, until the eighteenth-century Baumgarten was insisting that art, as an imitation of nature, arouses "sensuous knowledge," nothing more. During the materialistic nineteenth century this theory spread and hardened. Millions were now so absorbed in the earth and their own bodies they saw art as a matter of mere taste, or empathy, or sensation.

Yet the view of art as spirit-born never lost exponents. During that period Goethe called it not nature but nature as it might be; and Hegel argued that it belonged, no less than philosophy and religion, to the realm of the ideal. Most artists shared this viewpoint; to name a few, Blake, Tchaikovsky, Coleridge, Van Gogh, Tolstoy, Rodin. To the philosopher Schopenhauer intuition-based contemplation-causing art was a redemptive force freeing man from the tyranny of the will. And at the turn of the century Croce called it a language of the spirit fostering the unification of mankind.

Today the issue is more sharply drawn. Naturalism, the philosophy dominant in the West, has no room for God, the soul, immortality, freedom, or a theory of art as an influx of the spirit. But if materialism rages, the countermovement shows a mounting strength. To quote some representative spokesmen of our time: William Butler Yeats says that "the laws of art are the hidden laws of the world." T. E. Hulme (leaning on Worringer and echoed by Charles Williams) that there are two kinds of art, the nobler of which is non-objective, classical, "geometrical," spiritual. And the Swedish film director Ingmar Bergman: "It is my opinion that art lost its creative urge the moment it was separated from worship." Nor do artists stand alone in this controversy. The theologian Paul Tillich once told me that to him the closest synonym for "spirit" is "meaning" (and of course art is concentrated meaning); the psychologist Carl Jung that spirit lies behind the collective unconscious (and of course art reveals the unconscious).

Clearly Rudolf Steiner belongs to an age-old stream flowing sometimes aboveground, sometimes below, but never, since the beginning, dry.

In another sense he is unique; and these eight lectures touching on architecture, sculpture, painting, costuming, music, drama, poetry, and the new art of eurythmy, increase his extraordinary contribution to an ancient discussion. His frame of reference is nothing less than cosmic. Or say "the immanent space in the heart."

Here some warnings and reminders. These lectures have a looser construction than matter shaped originally for publication. Their movement is not the straight line of logic but the spiraling, the turning-back-upon-themselves-while-yet-going-forward, suitable for contents which, having to do with the spirit, ask for quiet musing, for meditation. Because he spoke to an audience familiar with his teachings, Dr. Steiner assumes a certain body of knowledge. And he never corrected the transcripts. Moreover, having dealt previously with other aspects, he does not pretend to cover all the problems of art; only certain key questions, informally. And most important: Though his findings are presented not as theory but realities discovered by direct spiritual perception, that is by looking behind the scenes of a "play played eternally before all creatures," they can be, and Dr. Steiner would say ought to be, judged strictly on their merits.

A reader with these facts in mind is better equipped to weigh what he finds here and nowhere else.

Reaffirming with the ancient Mysteries the inseparability of the good (morality), the true (science) and the beautiful (art)—three spheres connected not by likeness but analogy—Dr. Steiner stresses the aridity of matter-bound thinking and its enmity to art; and in the process makes points which, owing to absence of the pontifical manner, may deceive by their simplicity, may seem at first flush of limited scope when, actually, their implication for culture and the well-being of mankind reach out and out; for example (choosing at random), his statement that true architecture offers man the lines along which, when projected into the cosmos, the soul in life or death can expand; that true sculpture builds on the life-giving formative forces lying behind physical structure; that true painting relies on not spatial but color-perspective, color being an entire world in itself; that modern music, seeking depth in the single tone rather than in harmony or melody, begins, just begins, to find its way back to the spirit from which it descended; that poetry depends upon the relation between breath and pulse, nerve system and blood system; that eurythmy, as "expressive gesture," is linked with the invisible gesture-system which is language; and that imagination is the child's power of growth transformed for loftier purposes. . . .

Such insights can, by quickening creativity, multiply works "determined outwardly to use and inwardly to delight."

And perhaps such insights have a special significance for America. Elsewhere Dr. Steiner has observed that, to achieve balance, Russia needs philosophy, America art.

Virginia Moore

I

TODAY I propose to carry further certain points made in recent lectures concerning the evolution of humanity since the time of Christ.

Looking back, in survey, over the evolution of mankind, we see that the epochs described in anthroposophical spiritual science take their shape from the particular soul constitution of the human beings alive at any given time. This differs greatly from epoch to epoch. Today, however, there is little inclination to look beyond man's presentday makeup. Although civilization has developed in a way describable in outer documents, in general mankind is regarded as having always had the same soul nature. This is not true. It has changed; and we know the dates at which it underwent transformations externally plain and distinguishable.

The last of these turning points has often been designated as the fifteenth century after Christ; the one preceding it occurred during the eighth pre-Christian century; and we might in this way go still further back. I have often emphasized how correct the art historian Herman Grimm is when he points out that the full historical comprehension of the people of the present age reaches back no further than the Romans; at which time the ideas now prevalent settled into men's souls. Or approximately the same ideas. They still operate, though at times in a detrimental way—for example, concepts of Roman law no longer in harmony with our society. The very manner in which contemporary man takes part in social life shows a comprehension for something reaching back to the Roman period.

If, on the other hand, we describe the external historical events of ancient Greece like modern events, we do not penetrate into the real soul-nature of the Greeks. Herman Grimm is right in saying that, as usually described, they are mere shadows. Precisely because ordinary consciousness can no longer see what lived in those souls, it is unable to understand the Greeks' social structure.

Still more removed from our soul life is that of the human beings of the Egyptian-Chaldean period prior to the eighth century before Christ; more different still that in ancient Persia, and completely different that of the ancient Indian epoch following the great Atlantean catastrophe.

When with the help of spiritual science we mark the stages in the changing constitution of the human being, it becomes clear that our way of feeling about the human being, our way of speaking of body, soul and spirit, of the ego in man, our sense of an inner connection between the human being and the earth planet, arose in the fourth post-Atlantean epoch. Gradually, in the course of time, life has become so earth-bound that human beings feel estranged from the cosmos, and see the stars and their movements, even the clouds, as lying outside our earthly dwelling place; therefore of little significance.

Prior to the Graeco-Latin period, people's feelings and indeed their will-impulses were, if I may use the expression, elementary-cosmic. Man did not need a philosophy in order to feel himself a member of the whole universe, especially the visible universe. It was natural for him to feel himself not only a citizen of the earth but also a member of the cosmos. Especially during the first epoch, that of ancient India. If we go back to the seventh or eighth millennium of the pre-Christian era, we find that the human being—I cannot say *spoke* but *felt*—that the human being *felt* quite differently than we do today about the ego, the self. To be sure, the human beings of that ancient time did not express themselves as we do, because human speech did not have the same scope as today. But we must express things in our own language, and I shall put it thus: In ancient India man did not speak of the ego in our modern way; it was not, for him, a point comprising all his soul experiences. On the contrary, when he spoke of the ego it was to him self-evident that it had little to do with earth and earth-events. In experiencing himself as an ego, man did not feel that he belonged to the earth; but, rather, that he was connected with the heaven of the fixed stars. This was what gave him the sense and security of his deepest self. For it was not felt as a *human* ego. Man was a human being only through the fact that here on earth he was clothed by a physical body. Through this sheath-for-the-ego he became a citizen of earth. But the ego was regarded as something foreign to the earthly sphere. And if today we were to coin a name for the way the ego was experienced, we would have to say: man felt not a human but a divine ego.

He might have looked outward to the mountains, to the rocks; he might have looked at everything else on earth and said of it all: This is, this exists. Yet at the same time he would have felt the following: If there were no other existence than that of earth's plants, rivers, mountains and rocks, no human being would have an ego. For what guarantees existence to earthly things and beings could never guarantee it to the ego. They are in different categories.

To repeat: Within himself man felt not a human but divine ego: a drop from the ocean of divinity. And when he wanted to speak about his ego (I say this with the previously-made reservations) he felt it as a creation of the fixed stars; the heaven of the fixed stars was the one sphere sharing its reality. Only because the ego has a similar existence is it able to say, "I am." If it were able to say "I am" merely according to the level of existence of stone or plant or mountain, the ego would have no right to speak so. Only its starlike nature makes it possible for the ego to say, "I am."

Again, the human beings of this primeval epoch saw how the rivers flowed and the trees were driven by the wind. But if we regarded the human ego which dwells in the physical body and has an impulse to move about on the earth hither and thither—if we regarded this ego as the active force in movement, as wind is the active force in moving trees, or as anything else of earth is an active force, we would be wrong. The ego is not this kind of outer cause of motion.

In ancient times the teacher in the Mysteries spoke to his pupils somewhat like this: You see how the trees sway, how the river water flows, how the ocean churns. But from neither the moving trees, the flowing rivers, nor the heaving ocean could the ego learn to develop those impulses of motion which human beings display when they carry their bodies over the earth. This the ego can never learn from any moving earthly thing. This the ego can learn only because it is related to the planets, to starry motion. Only from Mars, Jupiter, Venus, and so forth, can the ego learn motion. When the ego of its own volition moves upon the earth, it achieves something made possible by its relation to the wheeling world of the stars.

Further, it would have seemed incomprehensible to a man of this ancient epoch if somebody had said: Look how thoughts arise out of your brain! Let us travel backward in time and imagine ourselves with the soul constitution we once had (for we have all passed through lives in ancient India); then confronted by the presentday soul condition, the one which makes people assume that thoughts arise out of the brain. All that modern man believes would appear as complete nonsense. For the ancient human being knew well that thoughts can never spring from brain substance; that it is the sun which calls forth thoughts, and the moon which stills them. It was to the reciprocal action of sun and moon that he ascribed his life of thoughts.

Thus in the first post-Atlantean epoch, the ancient Indian time, the divine ego was seen as belonging to the heaven of the fixed stars, to the planetary movements, to the reciprocal action of sun and moon; and what came to it from the earth as transient; the essence of the ego being cosmic-divine.

In *Occult Science** I call the second epoch Ancient Persian. By then the perception of the cosmic ego had grown less vivid; it was subdued. But the people of that age had an intensive experience of the recurrent seasons. (I have recently and repeatedly lectured on the year's course.) Pictorially speaking, the modern human being has become a kind of earthworm, just living from day to day. Indeed he is not even that, for an earthworm comes out of his hole when it rains, while the human being—just lives along. He experiences nothing special; at best some abstract differences: in rain he is uncomfortable without an umbrella, he adjusts himself to snow in winter and sunshine in summer, he goes to the country, and so forth. But he does not live with the course of the year; he lives in a dreadfully superficial way; no longer puts his whole humanness into living.

In the ancient Persian epoch it was different. Man experienced the year's course with his whole being. When the winter solstice arrived he felt: Now the earth soul has united with the earth. The snow which for presentday man is nothing but frozen water was at that time experienced as the garment the earth dons in order to shut itself off from

* Rudolf Steiner, *Occult Science, an Outline.* Anthroposophic Press, Inc., New York.

the cosmos and develop an individually-independent life within that cosmos. The human being felt: Now, indeed, the earth soul has so intimately united with the earth, man must turn his soul-nature to what lives in the earth. In other words, the snow cover became transparent for man's soul. Below it he felt the elementary beings which carry the force of plant-seeds through winter into spring.

When spring arrived in ancient Persia, man experienced how the earth breathed out its soul, how it strove to open its soul to the cosmos; and with his feelings and sensations he followed this event. The attachment to the earth developed during the winter he now began to replace with a devotion to the cosmos.

To be sure, man was no longer able to look up to the cosmos as he did during the immediately preceding epoch; no longer able to see in the cosmos all that gave existence, movement and thought to his ego. He said: What in winter unites me with the earth summons me in spring to raise myself into the cosmos. But though he no longer had so intensive a knowledge of his connection with the cosmos as formerly, he felt it as by divination. Just as the ego in the ancient Indian time experienced itself as a cosmic being, so in the ancient Persian time the astral element experienced itself as connected with the course of the year.

Thus man lived with the changing seasons. When in winter his soul perceived the snow blanket below, his mood turned serious; he withdrew into himself; searched (as we express it today) his conscience. When spring returned, he again opened himself to the cosmos with a certain gaiety. At midsummer, the time we now associate with St. John's Day, he surrendered with rapture to the cosmos, not in the clear way of the ancient Indian time, but with the joy of having escaped from the body.

Just as in winter he felt connected with the clever spirits

of the earth, so in midsummer he felt connected with the gay spirits dancing and jubilating in the cosmos, and flitting around the earth. I am simply describing what was felt.

Later, during August, and more especially September, the human soul felt it must now return to earth with the forces garnered from the cosmos during its summer withdrawal. With their help it could live more humanly during the winter season.

I repeat: It is a fact that during those ancient times man experienced the year's course with his whole being; considered its spiritual side as his own human concern.

He also felt the importance of training himself, at certain points of the year, in this intensive experience of the seasons; and such training bred impulses for the seasonal festivals. Later on, man would experience them only traditionally, only outwardly. But certain aspects would linger on. For example, the festivals of the summer and winter solstices would keep traces, but merely traces, of ancient, mighty and powerful experiences.

All this is connected with a revolution in the innermost consciousness of man. For ancient India it was quite impossible to speak of a "people," a "folk." Today this seems paradoxical; we find it hard to imagine that the feeling for such a thing arose only gradually. To be sure, the conditions of the earth made it necessary, even in the ancient Indian epoch, for inhabitants of the same territory to have closer ties than those living apart. But the concept of a people, the feeling of belonging to a folk, did not exist during the ancient Indian epoch.

Something different prevailed. People had a very vivid feeling for the succession of generations. A boy felt himself the son of his father, the grandson of his grandfather, the great-grandson of his great-grandfather. Of course, things were not dealt with the way we have to describe them with current concepts; but the latter are still appropriate. If we look into the mode of thought of that ancient time, we discover that within a family circle great emphasis was laid on an ability to enumerate one's forebears, grandfather, great-grandfather, great-great-grandfather, right down the line to very remote ancestors. A man felt himself as standing within this succession of generations.

As a consequence, the sense of living in the present was little developed. To human beings of the ancient Indian time, an intimate connection with past generations (retained as a caricature in aristocracy's presentday stress on ancestry) seemed self-evident; they needed no family records. Indeed human consciousness itself, instinctively clairvoyant, made connections with a man's ancestry by remembering not merely his own personal experiences, but—almost as vividly—the experiences of his father and grandfather. Gradually these memories grew dim. But human consciousness would continue to experience them through the blood ties.

Thus in ancient times the capacity for feeling oneself within the generations played a significant role. Parallel to it there arose—though slowly—the folk concept, the sense of being part of a people. In ancient Persia it was not yet very pronounced. When a living consciousness of life within the generations, of blood relationship coursing through the centuries, had gradually faded, consciousness focused, instead, on the contemporary folk relationship.

The folk concept rose to its full significance in the third post-Atlantean or Egypto-Chaldean period. Though, during that epoch, awareness of the year's course was already somewhat deadened, there lived, right into the last millennium of the pre-Christian age, a vivid consciousness of the fact that thoughts permeate and govern the world.

In another connection I have already indicated the following: For a human being of the Egyptian period the idea that thoughts arise in us and then extend over things outside would have seemed comparable to the fancy of a man who, after drinking a glass of water, says his tongue produced the water. He is at liberty to imagine that his tongue produced the water, but in truth he draws the water from the entire water mass of the earth, which is a unity. It is only that an especially foolish person, unaware of the connection between the glassful of water and the earth's water mass, overestimates the abilities of his tongue. The people of the Egypto-Chaldean epoch made no similar mistake. They knew that thoughts do not arise in the head; that thoughts live everywhere; that what the human being draws into the vessel of his head as thought comes from the thought ocean of the world.

In that time, though man no longer experienced the visible cosmos in his divine ego, nor the course of the year in his astral nature, he did experience cosmic thoughts, the Logos, in his etheric body. If a member of the Egypto-Chaldean epoch had spoken our language, he would not, like us, have referred to man's physical body as of prime importance. To him it was the result of what lives as thought in the etheric body; was merely an *image* of human thought.

During that period the folk concept became more and more definite; the human being more and more an earth citizen. The connection between the starry world and his ego had, in his consciousness during this third post-Atlantean cultural period, dwindled greatly. Though astrology still calculated the connection, it was no longer seen in elemental consciousness. The course of the year, so important for the astral body, was no longer sensed in its immediacy. Yet man was still aware of a cosmic thought element.

He had arrived at the point where he sensed his relation to earthly gravity. Not exhaustively so, for he still had a vivid experience of thinking, but perceptibly.

During the Graeco-Latin period this experience of gravity developed more and more. Now the physical body became paramount. Everything has its deep significance at its proper time, and in all the manifestations of Greek culture we see this full, fresh penetration into the physical body. Especially in Greek art. For the early Greeks their bodies were something to rejoice over; the Greeks were like children with new clothes. They lived in their bodies with youthful exuberance.

In the course of the Graeco-Latin period, and particularly during Roman civilization, this fresh experience of the physical body gave way to something like that of a person in a robe of state who knows that wearing it gives him prestige. (Of course, the feeling was not expressed in words.) A Roman individual felt his physical body as a ceremonial robe bestowed by the world order.

The Greek felt tremendous joy that he had been allotted such a body and, after birth, could put it on; and it is this feeling that gives to Greek art, to Greek tragedy, to the epics of Homer, in their human element, insofar as they are connected with the outer physical appearance of man, their particular poetic fire. We have to look for the inner reasons for all psychological facts. Try to live into the joy that gushes forth from Homer's description of Hector or of Achilles. Feel what immense importance he attached to outer appearance.

With the Romans this joy subsided. Everything became settled; men began to grasp things with ordinary consciousness. It was during the fourth post-Atlantean cultural epoch that man first became an earth citizen. The conception of ego, astral body and ether body of earlier times withdrew into indefiniteness. The Greeks still had a clear sense for the truth that thought lives in things. (I have discussed this in *Raetsel der Philosophie.*) But the perception was gradually superseded by a belief that thought originates in man. In this fashion he grew more and more into his physical body.

Today we do not yet see that this situation began to change in the fifteenth century, at the start of the fifth post-Atlantean cultural epoch; that, since then, we have been gradually growing away from our bodies. We fancy that we feel as the Greeks felt about the human shape, but actually our feeling for it is dull. We have no more than a shadowlike sensation of the "quickfooted Achilles," and little understanding of how this expression roused Greeks to a direct and striking perception of the hero; so striking that he stood before them in his essential nature. Indeed in all art we have gradually lost the experience of the permeation of the physical body by the soul; whereas in the last pre-Christian centuries the Greek felt how cosmic thought was disappearing and how thought could be taken hold of only by reflecting upon the human being. Presentday man is completely uncertain in regard to the nature of thought; he wavers.

A Greek of the sixth pre-Christian century would have considered it comical if somebody had asked him to solve the scientific problem of the connection of thought with the brain. He would not have seen it as a problem at all. He would have felt as we would feel if, when we picked up a watch, somebody demanded that we speculate philosophically about the connection between watch and hand. Say I investigate the flesh of my hand, then the glass and metal in my watch; then the relation between the flesh of my hand and the glass and metal in my watch; all in order to obtain philosophical insight into the reason why my hand has picked up and holds the watch. Well, if I were to proceed thus, modern consciousness would consider my gropings insane.

Just so it would have appeared insane to Greek consciousness if anyone had attempted, by reference to the nature of thought and the cerebellum, to explain the self-evident fact that man's being uses his brain to lay hold of thoughts. For the Greek this was a direct perception just as, for us, it is a direct perception that the hand takes hold of the watch; we do not consider it necessary to establish a scientific relation between watch and muscle. In the course of time problems arise according to the way things are perceived. For the Greek what we call the connection between thinking and organism was as self-evident as the connection between a watch and the hand that seizes it. He did not speculate about what was obvious. He knew instinctively how to relate his thoughts to himself.

If someone said: Well, there is only a hand; the watch ought to fall down, what really holds it? for the Greek this would have been as absurd as the question: What is it that develops thoughts in the brain? For us the latter has become a problem because we do not know that already we have liberated our thoughts, and are on our way to freeing them from ourselves. Also we do not know how to deal properly with thoughts because, being in the process of growing away from it, we no longer have a firm hold on our physical body.

I should like to use another comparison. We have not only clothes but pockets into which we can put things. This was the situation with the Greeks: their human bodies were something into which they could put thoughts, feelings, will impulses. Today we are uncertain what to do with thoughts, feelings and will impulses. It is as though, in spite of pockets, all our things fell to the ground; or as though, worried about what to do with them, we lugged them about in our hands. In other words, we are ignorant of the nature of our own organism, do not know what to do with our soul life in regard to it, contrive queer ideas with respect to psycho-parallelism, and so forth. I am saying all this to show how we have gradually become estranged from our physical bodies.

This fact is illustrated by the whole course of humanity's evolution. If we again turn our gaze to the ancient Indian time when the human being looked back through the succession of generations to a distant ancestor, we see that he felt no need to search for the gods anywhere but within the generations. Since, for the Hindu, man himself was divine, he remained within human evolution while looking for the divine in his forebears. Indeed the field of his search was precisely mankind's evolution.

There followed the time which culminated in the Egypto-Chaldean culture, when the folk concept rose to prominence and man beheld the divine in the various folk gods, in that which lived in blood relationships, not successively as before, but spatially side by side.

Then came the Greek period when man no longer felt god-imbued, when he became an earth citizen. Now for the first time there arose the necessity to seek the gods above the earth, to look up to the gods. By gazing at the stars, ancient man *knew* of the gods. But the Greek needed, in addition to the stars, the involvement of his personality in order to behold those gods; and this need kept increasing within mankind.

Today man must more and more develop the faculty of disregarding the physical, disregarding the physical starry sky, disregarding the physical course of the year, disregarding his sensations when confronting objects. For he can no longer behold his thoughts in matter. He must acquire the possibility of discovering the divine-spiritual as something special above and beyond the physical sense world before he can find it again within the sense world.

To emphasize this truth energetically is the task of anthroposophical spiritual science. Thus anthroposophical spiritual science grows out of the entire earthly evolution of mankind. We must always remember that Anthroposophy is not something arbitrarily created and placed as a program into mankind's evolution but, rather, something suited to our epoch, something resulting from the inner necessities of mankind's long history.

The fact that materialism hold sway over our age is, really, only a lagging behind. Man not only became an earth citizen in the Greek sense; today he is already so estranged from his earth citizenship he no longer understands how to handle his soul-spirit being in relation to his body—it is one of the needs of the age for the human being to behold spirit and soul in himself without the physical. Side by side with this deep soul-need, there exists materialism as an Ahrimanic stopping-short at something natural in the age of the Greeks and Romans when one could still behold the spiritual in the physical, but not natural today.

Having remained stationary, we can no longer see the spiritual in the physical; we consider only the physical as such. This is materialism. It means that a current hostile to development has entered evolution. Mankind shuns the coining of new concepts; it prefers to continue on with the old. We must overcome this hostility toward development; must open ourselves to it. Then we shall acquire a quite natural relationship to anthroposophical growth of spirit, and pass over from antiquated needs to the truly modern need of mankind: namely, to raise ourselves to the spiritual.

In today's lecture I have tried to gain a viewpoint from which you can see how, for the present age, in the evolution of mankind, Anthroposophy constitutes a real necessity.

II

ONE result of anthroposophical spiritual science—once it has been absorbed into civilization—will be a fructification of the arts. Precisely in our time the human inclination toward the artistic has diminished to a marked degree. Even in anthroposophical circles not everyone thoroughly comprehends the fact that Anthroposophy strives to foster, in every possible way, the artistic element.

This is of course connected with modern man's aforementioned aversion to the artistic. Today the positive way in which Goethe and many of his contemporaries sensed the unity of spiritual life and art is no longer experienced. Gradually the conception has arisen that art is something which does not necessarily belong to life, but is added to it as a kind of luxury. With such assumptions prevailing, the upshot is not to be wondered at.

In times when an ancient clairvoyance made for a living connection with the spiritual world, the artistic was considered absolutely vital to civilization. We may feel antipathy for the frequently pompous, stiff character of Oriental and African art forms; but that is not the point at issue. In this and further lectures we shall be concerned, not with our reaction to any particular art form, but rather with the way in which man's attitude places all the arts within the framework of civilization. The necessity is to see a certain connection between today's spiritual life and the attitude toward art previously alluded to.

If today, as is customary, one sees man as the highest product of nature, as a being brought forth at a certain point in earthly evolution (part of an evolutionary series fashioning a variety of beings), one falsifies the position of man in respect to the world; falsifies it because man has, in truth, no right to the self-satisfaction which would enter his soul, inevitably, as an elemental impulse of soul, if he were indeed only the terminal point of natural creation. If the animals had developed in the way currently assumed by natural science, then man, as the highest product of nature, would have to content himself with this status in the cosmos; he would have no call whatsoever to create something transcending nature.

For instance, if in art one wishes to create, as the Greeks did, an idealized human being, one has to be dissatisfied with what nature offers. For, if satisfied, one could never inject into nature something which surpasses her. Similarly, if satisfied with the nightingale's and lark's song, one could never compose sonatas and symphonies; such a combination of sounds would seem untrue; the true, the natural, being exhaustively expressed by the birds.

The naturalistic world-conception demands that those who wish to create something content themselves with imitations of the natural. For it is only when we envisage a world other than the natural one that we can see a transcending of nature as anything but dishonesty and sham.

We must grasp this fact. But presentday human beings do not draw the logical conclusion from naturalism as it affects the arts. What would happen if they did? They would have to demand that people imitate nature; nothing else. Well, but if a Greek prior to Aeschylos had been shown a mere imitation of nature, he would have said something like this: "Why all that? Why let actors speak as people do in everyday life? If you wish to hear such things, go into the street. Why present them on the stage? It is quite unnecessary. The street is a far better place to find out what people say to one another in ordinary life." In other words, only a person who participates in spiritual life has an impulse for a creative activity transcending the merely natural. Otherwise, where would the impulse come from? In all ages the human souls in which the artistic element flourished have had a definite relation to the spiritual world. It was out of a spirit-attuned state that the artistic urge proceeded. And this relation to the spiritual world will be, forever, the prerequisite for genuine creativity. Any age strictly naturalistic must, to be true to itself, become inartistic, philistine. Unfortunately our own age has an immense talent for philistinism.

Take the individual arts. Pure naturalism can never create an artistic architecture, a high art of building. Today the "art" of building leads away from art. For if people do not have a longing to assemble in places where the spiritual is fostered, they will not construct houses suitable for spiritual impulses, but merely utilitarian buildings. And what would they say of the latter? "Well," they would say, "we build in order to shelter our bodies, to protect the family; otherwise we would have to camp out in the open"—the idea of utility being primary. Though such an attitude is not, perhaps, because of embarrassment, generally admitted, it *is* admitted in particular cases. Today many people are offended if the architect of a residence sacrifices anything of expediency to the principle of the beautiful, the aesthetic; and one often hears the statement: "To build artistically is too expensive." People did not always think like that; certainly not in those ages when human souls experienced a kinship with the spiritual world. Then the feeling about man and his relation to the universe found expression in words somewhat like these: "Here I stand in the world, but as I stand here with a human form in which dwell soul and spirit, I carry within me something which has no existence in purely natural surroundings. When soul and spirit leave this body, then the relation between it and my physical environment will become manifest; this environment will consume my corporeal part. Only on a corpse do the laws of nature take effect." Which is to say that as long as the human being is not a corpse, as long as he lives here on earth, he can, through his spiritual heritage, through soul and spirit, preserve from the action of physicality the substances and forces which the corpse will eventually claim.

I have often remarked that eating is not the simple process ordinarily imagined. We eat, and the foods entering our organism are products of nature, natural substances and forces. Because they are foreign to us, our organism would not tolerate them if we could not transform them into something totally different. The energies and laws by means of which food is changed do not belong to the physical earthly environment. We bring them with us from another world. These facts and much else were recognized, understood, when people had a relationship with the spiritual world. Today, however, human beings think it is the laws of nature that are active in the roast beef when it rests on the plate, when it touches the tongue, when it has reached the stomach, intestines, blood; they see the laws of nature active everywhere. The fact that roast beef encounters spirit-soul laws which man himself has brought from another world into this one, and which transform it into something completely different —this fact has no place in the consciousness of a merely naturalistic civilization. Paradoxical as it may sound, materialists feel embarrassed to state bluntly the above. Yet they live with this attitude of mind.

It affects our whole artistic attitude. For, in the final analysis, why do we build houses for ourselves today? To be protected while eating roast beef! Well, this is only one detail. But all contemporary thinking tends in that direction.

By contrast, human beings of the past who had a living consciousness of their relationship to the spiritual universe erected their most valuable buildings to protect the human soul against inroads from their physical environment. Of course, when I use modern words in this connection they sound paradoxical. In ancient times people did not express themselves so abstractly. Things were felt, they were sensed subconsciously. But people's feelings, their unconscious sensations, were spiritual. Today we clothe these feelings in well-defined words which convey, not inadequately, what souls experienced in more ancient times. They were aware that, when a man has passed through an earth life, he lays aside his physical body; whereupon soul and spirit must find their way back into the spiritual universe. Consequently, these people were concerned as to how a soul fares after death: how it can find its way back into spiritual worlds.

Today people do not worry about such things, but there were times when this problem of *means* was a fundamental concern; when (for this is pertinent) people said to themselves: Outside, there are stones; outside, there are plants; outside, animals. When absorbed by man, substances derived from stones, plants, animals, are worked over by the physical body. Its spiritual forces can overcome some minerals—for example, salt. Similarly, it possesses the spirit-soul forces necessary for the overcoming of purely plant constituents, and can transform the animal element into the human element. All of which points up the fact that the physical body is a mediator between the human being who comes down from spiritual worlds and this so alien earth. Thanks to the physical body we can stand upon this earth; can exist among minerals, plants and animals.

But when the physical body has been laid aside, then the naked soul enters a state fitted only for the spiritual world; and having laid aside its body must ask: How can I pass through the impurity of the animals in order to escape from earthly regions? How pass through the plant element which absorbs, attracts and condenses light? How—accustomed to living amid earthly plant-condensed light—pass out into far reaches of quite another condition of light? How, when I can no longer dissolve them through body-juices, pass beyond the soul-impeding minerals massed on every side?

In ancient times, during mankind's evolution, these were religious-cultural anxieties. People pondered on what they had to do for souls, especially dear ones, to help them find the lines, planes, forms, by means of which they could reach the spiritual world. Thus was developed the art of erecting burial vaults, monuments, mausoleums, which embodied in their forms, their lines and planes, that which the discarnate soul requires if it is to be unimpeded by animals, plants and minerals when ready to find its way back to the spiritual world.

These edifices took their characteristic forms directly from the cult of the dead; and if we wish to comprehend how they arose, we must try to understand how the soul, deprived of its body, finds its way back to the spiritual world of its origin. The belief prevailed that, because the soul has a certain relation to the discarded body, it can find the path out into the world of spirit through the architectural forms vaulting above it.

This conviction was one of the fundamental impulses behind the development of ancient architectural forms. Insofar as these forms were artistic and not merely utilitarian, they took their rise from edifices for the dead. In other words, artistic construction was intimately connected with the cult of the dead; or, as in the case of Greece, with the fact that each temple was built for Athena, Apollo or some other god. For just as the human soul was thought to be incapable of unfolding amid minerals, plants and animals, so the divine-spiritual natures of Apollo, of Zeus, of Athena, were thought to be incapable of unfolding amid external nature unless the spirit of man created for them certain congenial forms. Only if we study the way the soul is related to the cosmos can we understand measurements and proportions in the complicated architectural forms of the ancient Orient; forms which are living proof of the fact that the human beings from whose imaginations they sprang said to themselves: "Man in his inner being does not belong to the earth; he is of another world, therefore needs forms which belong to him in his character as a native of that other world."

No true historical art form can be understood from merely naturalistic principles. To understand we must ask: What lies behind and is inherent in it? For example, here is the human body, the indwelling human soul. The soul, through its

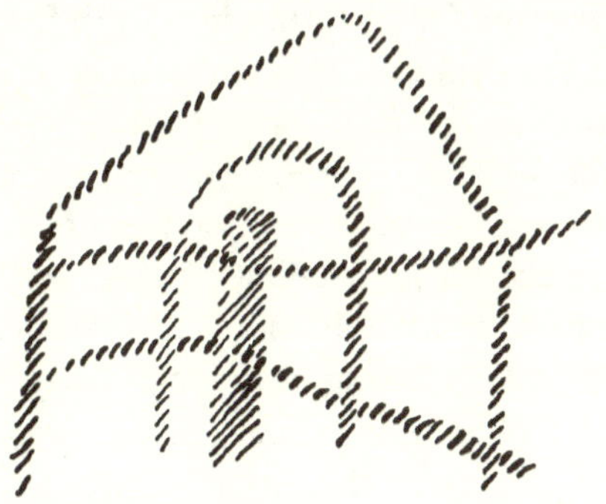

inherent nature, desires to unfold in all directions; and the way it would unfold, disregarding the body, the way it desires to carry its being out into the cosmos, becomes an architectural form.

O soul, if you wish to leave the physical body in order to

regain a relationship with the cosmos, what aspect will you take on?—this was the question. The forms of architecture were, so to speak, answers.

Within the evolution of mankind this impulse toward outer expression of inner needs continued to work for a long time. But of course today, during the age of abstractions, everything takes on a different appearance. Which does not mean that we should wish to retrieve the past; only to understand it.

Another custom of the past, though not a very ancient past, asking to be understood: churches surrounded by graves. Not every person could have an individual tomb; the church was the common mausoleum. Therefore it was the church which had to answer, through its form, the ancient question of the soul: How unfold, how escape in the right way, from the body connecting me with the physical world? Ecclesiastical architecture bodies forth, as it were, the desire of the soul for its right after-death form.

To repeat: past cultural elements can be understood only in connection with the feelings and intuitions which people had out of the spiritual world. To understand a cemetery-surrounded church we must develop a sense for the feelings which lived in the original builders when they asked: Dear souls leaving us in death, what forms do you wish us to erect so that, while still hovering near your body, you can take them on and be helped? The answer was ecclesiastical architecture, the artistic element in which was directed toward the end of earth life. Certainly, all this undergoes a metamorphosis. What proceeds from the cult of the dead can become the highest expression of life (as in what we attempted for the Goetheanum). But one must understand things; must understand that architecture unfolds out of the principle of the soul's escape from the body, out of the principle of the soul's growing beyond the body, after passing through the portal of death.

And if we look in the opposite direction, toward birth, toward man's passage from the spiritual into the physical world, then I must tell you something which may make you smile, a little, inwardly; or, perhaps, you won't smile; in which case I would say, Thank goodness! For what I am going to say is true. You see, when the soul arrives on earth in order to enter its body, it has come down from spirit-soul worlds in which there are no spatial forms. Thus the soul knows spatial forms only after its bodily experience, only while the after-effects of space still linger on.

But though the world from which the soul descends has no spatial forms or lines, it does have color intensities, color qualities. Which is to say that the world man inhabits between death and a new birth (and which I have frequently and recently described) is a soul-permeated, spirit-permeated world of light, of color, of tone; a world of qualities, not quantities; a world of intensities rather than extensions. Thus in certain primitive, almost-forgotten civilizations, he who descended and dipped into a physical body had the sensation that through it he entered into relation with a physical environment, grew into space. To him the physical body was completely attuned to space, and he said to himself: "This is foreign to me, it was not so in the spirit-soul world. Here I am under the joke of three dimensions—dimensions which had no meaning before my descent into the physical world. But color, tone harmonies, tone melodies, have very much meaning in the spiritual world."

In those ancient epochs when such realities were sensed, man had a strong desire not to take into his being what was essentially foreign to him. At his most perceptive, he sensed that his head had been given him by the spiritual world. For, as I have often remarked, our trunk and limbs in one life become our head in the next; and so on, from life to life. Ancient man felt the adjustment of his lower body to gravity, to the forces circling the earth; felt its imprisonment in space; and felt that what entered his physical body from his environment did not befit him as a human being bearing, within, an impulse from spiritual worlds. He must do something to bring about a harmonization with his new home.

That was why he carried down from spiritual worlds the colors of his garments. Just as, in ancient times, architecture pointed to the end of earth life, to the death-pole, so in times when man had a sense for the artistic meaning of the colors and styles of dress, the art of costuming pointed to the beginning of human life, to the birth-pole.

Thus (I repeat) ancient garments reflected something brought down from pre-earthly existence, reflected a predilection for the colorful, for harmony; and we need not be astonished that at a time when insight into the pre-earthly has withered, the art of costuming has shriveled into dilettantism. For modern clothing hardly conveys the feeling that man wants to wear it because of the way he lived in pre-earthly existence. But if you study the characteristically vivid garments of flourishing primitive cultures you will see that clothing is or can be a fully justified and great art through which man carries something of his pre-earthly life into earth life; just as, through architecture, he would receive impressions relevant to space-free, post-earthly conditions.

Peoples who still wear national costumes express, through them, the pre-earthly relationships which led them into a certain folk community. Their garments remember, as it were, their appearance in heaven.

Often, to find meaningful costumes, you must go back to more ancient times. And you will see not only that there flourished, then, painters, sculptors, and so forth, but that people of other occupations, during the whole period, were highly artistic.

If you look at Raphael's paintings, you will see that Mary Magdalene and the Virgin Mary are clothed quite differently; also that in all his works Raphael gives Mary Magdalene—essentially—her characteristic garment, and the Virgin Mary hers. He did this because he still experienced in living tradition the fact that a soul-spirit being, brought down from heaven, expresses himself through his garments.

Here lies the meaning of costuming. Modern man may say that clothes derive significance through the fact that they provide warmth. Well, certainly, that is one of their materialistic meanings. But it creates no aesthetic forms. Artistry arises always and only through a relation to the spiritual.

This mode in which things stand to the spiritual must be found again if we would penetrate to the truly artistic. And since Anthroposophy takes hold of the spiritual in its immediacy, it can have a fructifying influence upon art. The great secrets of the world and of life which must be revealed out of anthroposophical research will prove to be artistic; will culminate in art.

In this connection we must perceive something anatomical, already referred to. That part of the human organism which was not head during one earth-life transforms itself, dynamically, into head in the subsequent life. Then (this is self-evident) it is filled out with earth-substance. I have often explained that we must not make the silly objection: The physical body having perished, how can a head arise from it? The other objections brought against Anthroposophy are not, as a rule, much more clever; and this one is really cheap. But we are not concerned, here, with the physical filling out; only with a force relationship which can pass through the spiritual world. The relationship of forces which today inheres in all parts of our physical organism below the head (whether those forces move vertically or horizontally, whether they are held together or expand) has a spherical tendency, becoming thereby the force relationship of our head in our next earth life. When the metamorphosis of legs, feet and so forth into head takes place, the higher hierarchies cooperate. For all heavenly spirits work together. Small wonder, then, that the top of the head appears as an image of the vast

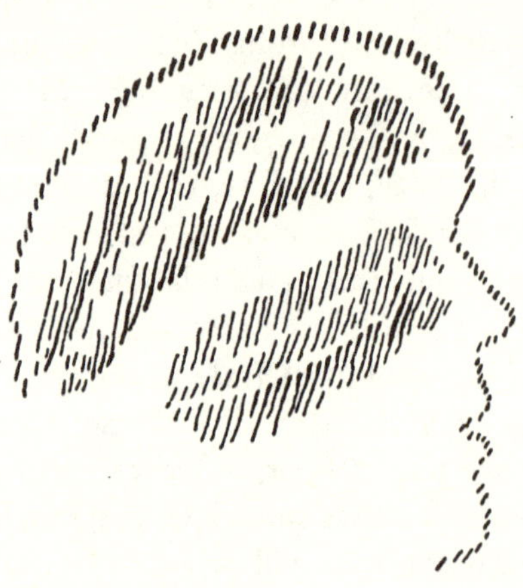

space arching spherically above us. And that the adjacent area is an image of the atmosphere circling round the earth; of atmospheric forces. One might say: In the upper part of the head we have a faithful image of the heavens; in the middle, an adaptation of the head to forces which triumph in the chest, to all that encircles the earth. For in our chest we need the earth-encircling air, need the light weaving round the earth, and so forth. The whole organism below the head has no form relationship to the head's spherical form—it has a relationship of substance, not of form; but our chest has a definite relationship to our nose, indeed to everything pertaining to the middle part of the head. And if we descend to the mouth, we find that it is related to the third member of the human threefoldness, namely, to the organism devoted to digestion, nutrition, and motion.

We see how what has passed through the heavens to become head on earth (out of the previous headless body-formation) is in its majestic spherical form adapted to the heavens; whereas the middle part comes from what man is through earth-encircling orbits; and the mouth's formation from what earthly man is through earthly substance and the power of gravity.

Thus, in terms of European mythology, the head of the human being contains, above, as it were, *Asgard,* the castle of the gods; in its middle part, *Midgard,* man's earthly home; and, below, what also belongs to the earth, *Jotunheim,* home of the giants.

These interrelationships do not become clear through abstract concepts; they become clear only if we perceive the human head artistically, in relation to its spiritual origin; only when we see in it heaven, earth and hell. Not hell as the abode of the devil; hell as the home of the giants, *Jotunheim.* There lives in the head the entire human being: a whole.

We look at a person in the right way if we see in the spherical form of the upper part of the head the purest memory of his previous incarnation; if we see in the middle part, in the lower portion of the eyes and in nose and ears, a memory dulled by the atmosphere of earth; and in the formation of the mouth, that part of his previous human formation conquered by earth, banished to earth. In the configuration of his forehead the human being brings with him, in a certain sense, what has been passed on to him karmically from his previous earth-life. In the formation of his chin he is conquered by the earthly life of the present age; he expresses gentleness or obstinacy in his chin formation. If his previous organization, minus head, had not transformed itself into his present head, he would not have a chin at all. But in the formation of mouth and chin all current earth impulses are so strong that they press and constrain the past into the present.

Therefore no artistic person will say: That human being is striking because of his prominent forehead. Rather, he will pay special attention to its spherical shape, to the formation of its planes. Its protrusion or recession is less important than its spherical shape.

In regard to the chin he will say: It is advancing, obstinate and pointed; or: It gently recedes. Here we begin to understand the form of man out of the whole universe; not merely out of the present universe—there we find little—but out of the temporal universe, then the extra-temporal.

Thus through anthroposophical considerations we are driven toward the artistic element, and see that philistinism is in no way compatible with a true and living apprehension of Anthroposophy. That is why inartistic people find it so difficult to come into harmony with the whole of this teaching. Though, abstractly, they might with pleasure recognize their present life as the fulfillment of previous earth lives, they are unable to enter intimately into the forms which reveal themselves in direct artistic fashion to spiritual perception, creating and transforming: a necessary activity for anyone desiring to unite with the essential living anthroposophical element.

This is the foundation I wished to lay down in order to show how the unspiritual character of our time manifests in the most varied spheres; among others, in a widespread unspiritual attitude toward art. If mankind desires to save itself from the unspiritual, one factor in its rescue will be a reversal of this position.

A true life in the artistic: to this desirable end Anthroposophy can show the way.

III

YESTERDAY I tried to show how the anthroposophical world-conception stresses, more intensively than is possible under the influence of materialism, the artistic element; and how Anthroposophy feels about architecture, about the art of costuming (though this may call forth smiles), and about sculpture as dealing artistically with the form of man himself, whose head, in a certain sense, points to the whole human being.

Let us review the most important aspects of this threefold artistic perception of the world. In architectural forms we see what the human soul expects when it leaves the physical body at death or otherwise. During earth life the soul is (so I said) accustomed to enter into spatial relations with its environment through the physical body, and to experience spatial forms. But these are only outer forms. When at death the human soul leaves the physical world, it tries, as it were, to impress its own form on space; looks for the lines, planes and forms which can enable it to grow out of space and into the spiritual world. These are the forms of architecture insofar as they are artistic. Thus, if we would understand architecture's artistic element we must consider the soul's space-needs after it has left the three-dimensional body and three-dimensional world.

The artistic element in costuming represents something else; and I have described the joy of primitive people in their garments, and their sense—on dipping down into the physical body—of finding in it a sheath which did not harmonize with what they had experienced during their sojourn in the spiritual world; and how out of this deprivation there arose an instinctive longing to create clothes which in color and pattern corresponded to their memory of pre-earthly existence. The costumes of primitive peoples represent what might be called an unskillful copying of the astral nature of man as it existed before he entered earthly life.

Thus a contrast. Whereas architecture shows the human soul's striving on its departure from the body, the art of costuming shows the human soul's striving after descent into the physical world.

Which brings us to a consideration of sculpture.

If we feel, intimately, the significance of the formation of man's head (my last point yesterday) as a metamorphosis of his entire body formation minus head, during his previous incarnation; if we see it as the work of the higher hierarchies on the force relationship of a previous life, then we understand the head, especially its upper part. If, on the other hand, we see correctly the middle of man's head, his nose and lower eyes, then we understand how this part is adapted to his chest formation, for the nose is connected with the chest's breathing. And if we see correctly the lower head, mouth and chin, then we understand that, even in the head, there is a part adapted to the purely earthly. In this way we can understand the whole human form. Furthermore, the supersensible human being manifests himself directly in the arching of the upper skull, and the protrusion or recession of the lower skull, the facial parts. For an intimate connection exists between the vaulting of the head and the heavens; also an inner connection between the middle of the face and everything circling the earth as air and ether; also between mouth-and-chin and man's limb and metabolic system, the last an indication of how man is fettered to earth. In this way we can understand the whole human form as an imprint of the spiritual on the immediate present; which means seeing man artistically.

To sum up: in sculpture we behold, spiritually, the human being as he is placed into the present; in architecture we behold something connected with his departure from the body; and in the art of costuming something connected with his entrance into that body. Which means a sharp contrast: whereas architecture begins with the erection of tombs, sculpture shows how man, through his earthly form's direct participation in the spiritual, constantly overcomes the earthly-naturalistic element, how, in every detail of his form and in its entirety, he is an expression of the spiritual.

Thus we have considered those arts which are concerned with spatial forms and which illustrate the different ways in which the human soul is related to the world through the physical body.

If we approach a step nearer the spaceless, we pass from sculpture to painting, an art experienced in the right way only if we take into full account its special medium.

Today, in the fifth post-Atlantean age, painting has assumed a character leading to naturalism. Its prime manifestation is the loss of a deeper understanding for color. The intelligence employed in contemporary painting is a falsified sculptural one. Painters see even human beings this way. The cause is space-perspective, an aspect of painting developed only after the fifth post-Atlantean period. Painters express through lines the fact that something lies in the background, something in the foreground; their purpose being to conjure up on canvas an impression of spatially formed objects. But in doing so they deny the first and foremost attribute of their special medium. A true painter does not create in space, but on the plane, in color, and it is nonsense for him to strive for the spatial.

Please, do not believe me so fantastic as to object to a feeling for space; in the evolution of mankind the development of spatial perspective on the plane was a necessity; that fact is self-evident. But it must now be overcome. This does not mean that in the future painters should be blind to spatial perspective, only that, while understanding it, they should return to color-perspective, employ color-perspective.

To accomplish this we must go beyond theoretic comprehension; the artistic impulse does not spring from theory; it requires something more forceful, something elemental. Fortunately it can be provided. For that purpose I suggest that you look again at some words of mine about the world of color as reported excellently by Albert Steffen in the weekly *Das Goetheanum.** (The report reads better than the original lectures.) This is the first aspect.

I shall now deal with the second problem.

In nature we see objects which can be counted, weighed and measured; in short, objects dealt with in physics. They appear in various colors. Color, however—this should have become perfectly clear to anthroposophists—color is something spiritual. Now we do see colors in certain natural entities which are not spiritual; that is, in minerals. Recent physicists have made matters easier for themselves by saying that colors cannot inhere in dead substances because colors are mental; they exist within the mind only; outside, material atoms vibrating in dead matter affect eye, nerve, and something else undetermined; as a result of which colors arise in the soul.

This explanation shows physicists at a loss in regard to the problem of color. To throw light on it, let us consider from a certain aspect the colorful dead mineral world.

As pointed out, we do see colors in purely physical things

* Vol. II, 1922, No. 7-9: *Vortraege Rudolf Steiner's ueber das Wesen der Farbe,* (Rudolf Steiner's Lectures Concerning the Nature of Color.)

which can be counted, measured, weighed on scales. But what is perceived in physics does not give us colors. We may employ number, measure and weight to our heart's content: we will not arrive at color. That is why physicists say that colors exist only in the mind.

I would like to explain by way of an image. Picture to yourselves that I hold in my left hand a red sheet, in my right a green one, and that with these colored sheets I carry out certain movements. First I cover the red with the green, then the green with the red, making these motions alternately; and in order to give them more character do something additional: move the green upward, the red downard. Say I have today carried out this maneuvre. Now let three weeks pass, at which time I bring before you not a green and red sheet, but two white sheets, and repeat the movements. You immediately remember that, contrary to my present use of white sheets, three weeks ago I produced certain visual impressions with a red and a green sheet. For politeness' sake let us assume that all of you have such a vivid imagination that, in spite of my moving white sheets, you see before you, through recollecting phantasy, the colored phenomenon of three weeks ago, forget all about the white sheets and, because I carry out the same motions, see the same color harmonies called forth, three weeks ago, with the red and green. Because I carry out the same gestures, by association you see what you saw three weeks ago.

The case is similar when we see in nature, for instance, a green precious stone. Only, the jewel is not dependent on this moment's soul-phantasy; it appeals to a phantasy concentrated in our eye, for this human eye with its blood and nerve fibers is in truth constructed by phantasy; it is the result of an effective imagination. And inasmuch as our eye is an organ imbued with phantasy, we cannot perceive a green gem in any other way than that in which, in the immeasurably distant past, it was spiritually constructed out of the green color of the spiritual world. The moment we confront a green precious stone, we transport our eye back into ages long past, and green appears because at that time divine-spiritual beings created this substance through a purely spiritual green. The moment we see green, red, blue, yellow, or any other color in a precious stone, we look back into an infinitely distant past. For (to repeat for emphasis) in beholding colors, we do not merely perceive what is contemporary, we look back into distant time-perspectives. Thus it is quite impossible to see a colored jewel merely in the present, just as it is impossible, while standing at the foot of a mountain, to see in close proximity the ruin at its top; being removed from it, we have to see it in perspective.

In confronting a topaz, say, we look back into time-perspective; look back upon the primal foundation of earthly creation, before the Lemurian epoch of evolution, and see this precious stone created out of the spiritual; that is why it appears yellow. Physics (I have characterized a recent stand) does something absurd. It places behind the world swirling atoms which are supposed to produce colors within us, when all the time it is divine-spiritual beings, creative in the infinitely distant past, who call forth, through colored minerals, a living memory of primeval acts of creativity.

And we can press on to the plant world.

Every spring, when a green carpet of plants is spread over the earth, whoever is able to understand this emergence of greenness sees not merely the present, but also the ancient Sun existence when the plant world was created out of the spiritual, in greenness. We see both mineral and plant colors in the right way when they stimulate us to see in nature the gods' primeval creative activity.

This requires an artistic living with color, which involves experiencing the plane as such. If someone covers the plane with blue, we should sense a retreat, a drawing back; if with red or yellow, we should feel an approach, a pressing forward. In other words, we acquire color-perspective instead of linear perspective: a sense for the plane, for the withdrawal and surging forward of color. In painting, the linear perspective which tries to create an impression of something essentially sculptural upon the plane falsifies; what must be acquired is a sense for the movement of color: intensive rather than extensive. Thus, if a true painter wishes to depict something aggressive, something eager to jump forward, he uses yellow-red; if something quiet, something retreating into the distance, blue-violet. Intensive color-perspective! A study of the old masters reveals that some early Renaissance painters still had what belonged to all pre-Renaissance painters: a feeling for color-perspective. Only with the advent of the fifth post-Atlantean period did linear perspective displace color-perspective.

It is through color-perspective that painting gains a relationship to the spiritual. Strange that today painters chiefly ask themselves: Can we by rendering space more spatial transcend space? Then they try to depict, in a materialistic manner, a fourth dimension. But the fourth dimension can exist only through annihilation of the third, somewhat as debts annihilate wealth. For we do not, on leaving three-dimensional space, enter a four-dimensional space; or, better said, we enter a four-dimensional space which is two-dimensional, because the fourth dimension annihilates the third; only two remain as reality. If we rise from matter's three dimensions to the etheric element, we find everything oriented two-dimensionally, and can understand the etheric only if we conceive of it so. Now you may demur: Yes, but in the etheric I move from here to there, which is to say three-dimensionally. Very well, but the third dimension has no significance for the etheric, only the other two dimensions. The third dimension expresses itself through red, yellow, blue, violet, in the way explained; for in the etheric it is not the third dimension which changes, but color. Regardless of where the plane is placed, the colors change accordingly. Only then can we live with and in color; live two-dimensionally; rise from the spatial arts to those which, like painting, are two-dimensional. We overcome the merely spatial. Our feelings have no relation to the three space-dimensions; only our will. By their very nature, feelings are bound within two dimensions. That is why they are best represented by two-dimensional painting.

You see, we have to struggle free from three-dimensional matter if we would advance from architecture, costuming as an art, and sculpture. Painting is an art which man can experience inwardly. Whether he creates as a painter or just lives in and enjoys a painting, it is a soul event. He experiences inner by outer; experiences color-perspective. We cannot say, as in the case of architecture, that the soul is striving to create the forms it needs when it gazes back into the body; nor, as in the case of sculpture, that the soul is trying to depict man's shape in such a way that it is placed into space full of present meaning. None of this concerns painting. It makes no sense in painting to speak of anything as inside or outside; of the soul as inside or outside. In experiencing color the soul is within the spiritual. Really, what is experienced in painting—despite the imperfections of pigments—is the soul's free moving about in the cosmos.

With music it is different. Now we do not merge inner with outer, but enter directly into that which the soul experiences as the spiritual or psycho-spiritual; leave space entirely. Music is line-like, one-dimensional; is experienced one-dimensionally in the line of time. In music man experiences the world as his own. Now the soul does not assert something it needs upon descending into or leaving the physical; rather it experiences something which lives and vibrates here and now, on earth, in its own soul-spirit nature. Studying the secrets of music, we can discover what the Greeks, who knew a great deal about these matters, meant by the lyre of Apollo. What is experienced musically is really man's hidden adaptation to the inner harmonic-melodic relationships of cosmic existence out of which he was shaped. His nerve fibers, ramifications of the spinal cord, are marvelous musical strings with a metamorphosed activity. The spinal cord culminating in the brain, and distributing its nerve fibers throughout the body, is the lyre of Apollo. Upon these nerve fibers the soul-spirit man is "played" within the earthly sphere. Thus man himself is the world's most perfect instrument; and he can experience artistically the tones of an external musical instrument to the degree that he feels this connection between the sounding of strings of a new instrument, for example, and his own coursing blood and nerve fibers. In other words, man, as nerve man, is inwardly built up of music, and feels it artistically to the degree that he feels its harmonization with the mystery of his own musical structure.

Thus, in devoting himself to the musical, man appeals to his earth-dwelling soul-spirit nature. The discovery by anthroposophical vision of the mysteries of this nature will have a fructifying effect, not just on theory, but upon actual musical creation.

In discussing the various arts I have not been theorizing. It is not theorizing when I say: In beholding the lifeless material world in color we stir cosmic memory; and through anthroposophical vision learn to understand how in precious stones, in colored objects of all kinds, we call to mind the creative acts of the primordially active gods; and feel, therefore, the enthusiasm which only an experience of the spiritual kindles. This is no theorizing; this permeates the soul with inner force. Nor does any theory of art emerge therefrom. Only artistic creation and enjoyment are stimulated. For true art is an expression of man's search for a relationship with the spiritual, whether the spiritual longed for when his soul leaves the body, or the spiritual which he desires to remember when he dips down into a body, or the spiritual to which he feels more related than to his natural surroundings, or the spiritual as manifested in colors when outside and inside lose their separateness and the soul moves through the cosmos, freely, swimming and hovering, as it were, experiencing its own cosmic life, existing everywhere; or (our last consideration) the spiritual as expressed in earth life, in the relationship between man's soul-spirit and the cosmic, in music.

Which summary brings us to the world of poetry and drama.

Often in the past I have called attention to the way poetry was felt in ancient times when man still had a living relationship to the spirit-soul world, when poetry, including poetic dramas, by reason of that fact, was artistic through and through. Yesterday I pointed out that in artistic ages it would not have been considered sensible for playwrights to copy on the stage the way Smith and Jones move in the market place of Gotham or at home, inasmuch as their movements and conversation, there, are much richer than in any stage representation; that it would have seemed absurd, for instance, to the Greeks of the classical age; they never could have understood naturalism's strange attempt to imitate nature right down to "realistic" stage sets. Just as it would not be true painting if we tried to project color into three-dimensional space instead of honoring its own dynamics, so it is not stage art if we have no artistic feeling for its own particular medium. Actually a thorough-going naturalism would preclude a stage room with three walls and an audience in front of it. There are no such rooms; in winter we would freeze to death in them. To act entirely naturalistically one would have to close the stage with a fourth wall and play behind it. But how many people would buy tickets to a play enacted on a stage closed on four sides? Though speaking in extremes, I refer to a reality.

Now I must draw your attention again to the way Homer begins his *Iliad*: "Sing, oh Goddess, the wrath of Achilles, Son of Peleus." This is no mere phrase. Homer experienced in a positive way the need to raise himself up to the level of a super-earthly divine-spiritual being who would make use of

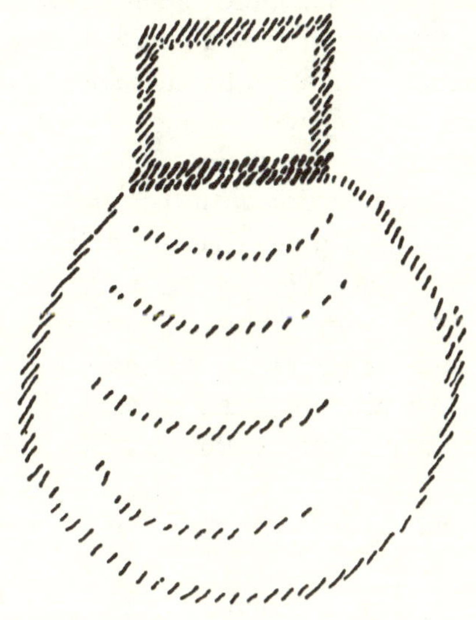

his body in artistic creation. Epic poetry points to the upper gods, those considered female because they transmitted fructifying forces: the Muses. Homer had to offer himself up to these upper gods in order to bring to expression, in the events of his great poem, the thought element of the cosmos. Epic poetry always means letting the upper gods speak; means putting one's person at their disposal. Homer begins his *Odyssey* this way: "Tell me, oh Muse, of that ingenious hero who wandered afar," meaning Odysseus. Never would it have occurred to him to impose upon the people something which he himself had seen or thought out. Why do what everybody can do for himself? Homer put his organism at the disposal of the upper divine-spiritual beings that they might express through him how they perceived earthly human relationships. Out of such a collaboration arises epic poetry.

And the art of the drama? It originated—we need only to think of the period prior to Aeschylus—from a presentation of the god Dionysus working up out of the depths. At first it was Dionysus alone, then Dionysus and his helpers, a chorus grouped around him as a reflection of what is carried out, not by human beings, but by the subterranean gods, gods of will, making use of human beings to bring to manifestation not the human but divine will. Only gradually, in Greece, as man's connection with the spiritual fell into oblivion, did the divine action depicted on the stage turn into purely human action. The process took place between the time of Aeschylus, when divine impulses still penetrated human beings, and the time of Euripides, when men appeared on the stage as men, though still bearing super-earthly impulses. Real naturalism became possible only in modern times.

In poetry and drama man must find his way back to the spiritual.

Thus we may say in summary: Epic poetry turns to the upper gods, drama to the lower gods. True drama shows the divine world lying below the earth, the chthonic world, rising up onto the earth for the reason that man can make himself into an instrument for the action of this netherworld. In contrast, epic poetry sees the upper spiritual world sink down; the Muse descends and, making use of man through his head, proclaims man's earthly accomplishments or else those out in the universe. In drama the subterranean will of the gods rises up from the depths, making use of human bodies in order to give free reign to their wills.

One might say: Here we have the fields of earthly existence; out of the clouds descends the divine Muse of epic art; out of earthly depths there rise, like vapor and smoke, the Dionysian, chthonic divine-spiritual powers, working their way upward through men's wills. We have to penetrate earth regions to see how the dramatic element rises like a volcano, and the epic element sinks down from above, like a blessing

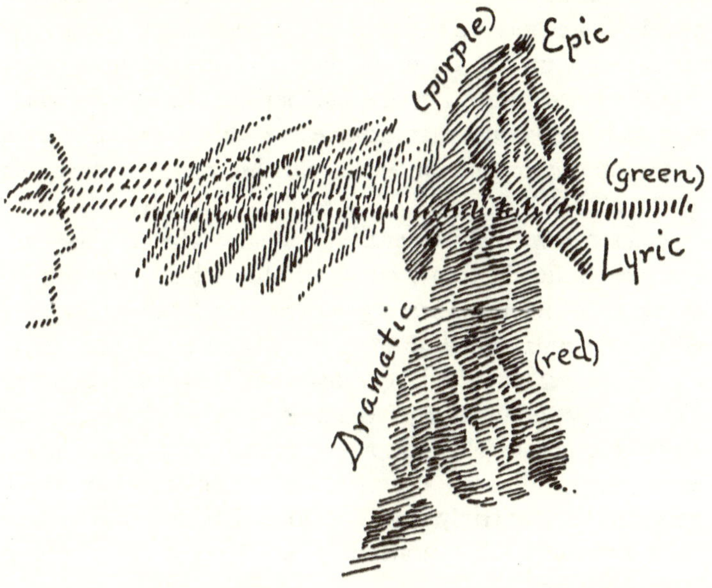

of rain. And it is right here on this same plane with ourselves that the cosmic element is enticed and made gay, joyous, full of laughter, through nymphs and fire spirits; right here that the messengers of the upper gods cooperate with the lower; right here in the middle region that man becomes lyrical. Now man does not feel the dramatic element rising up from below, nor the epic element sinking down from above; he experiences the lyrical element living on the same plane as himself: a delicate, sensitive, spiritual element, which does not rain down upon forests nor erupt like volcanoes, splitting trees, but, rather, rustles in leaves, expresses joy through blossoms, wafts gently in wind. In whatever on our own plane lets us divine the spiritual in matter, stretching hearts, pleasantly stimulating breath, merging our souls with outer nature, as symbol of the soul-spiritual world—in all this there lives and weaves a lyrical element which looks up, with happy countenance, to the upper gods, and down, with saddened countenance, to the gods of the underworld. The lyrical can tense up into the dramatic-lyrical or quiet itself down into the epic-lyrical. For the hallmark of the lyrical, whatever its form, is this: man experiences what lives and weaves in the far reaches of the earth with his middle nature, his feeling nature.

You see, if we really enter the spirituality of world phenomena, we gradually transform dead abstract concepts into a living, colorful, form-bearing weaving and being. Because what surrounds us lives in the artistic, mere intellectual activity can, almost unnoticed, be transformed into artistic activity. That is why we constantly feel a need to enliven impertinently abstract conceptual definitions—physical body, ether body, astral body, all such concepts, these impertinently rigid, philistine and horribly scientific formulations—into artistic color and form. This is an inner, not merely outer, need of Anthroposophy.

Therefore the hope may be expressed that all mankind will extricate itself from naturalism, drowned as it is in philistinism and pedantry through everything abstract, theoretical, merely scientific, practical without being really practical. Man needs a new impetus. Without this impulse, this swing, Anthroposophy cannot thrive. In an inartistic atmosphere it goes short of breath; only in an artistic element can it breathe freely. Rightly understood, it will lead over to the genuinely artistic without losing any of its cognitional character.

IV

THE LAST two lectures concentrated on artistic feeling and creation. I wished to call attention to the fact that anthroposophical contemplation leads to a particular manner of beholding the world, which must lead, in turn, to an inner vitalization of the arts, present and future. At the end of yesterday's lecture I stressed the fact that, by gaining a direct relation to the spiritual, a person can acquire the forces necessary for the creation, out of his innermost core, of true art. It has always been so. For true art stands beside real knowledge on the one hand, and on the other, genuine religious life. Through knowledge and religion man draws closer to the spiritual element in thought, feeling and will. Indeed, it is his inward experience of knowledge and religion, during ar. earth life, that brings about a sense of the validity of all that I discussed during the last two lectures. Looking at the physical surroundings akin to his physical body, he comes to realize that physicality is not the whole of his humanness. In all artistic and religious ages he has recognized this truth, saying to himself: Though I stand within earth existence, it contradicts that part of my human nature which was imaged forth from worlds quite different from the one in which I live between birth and death.

Let us consider this feeling I have just described in respect to cognition. Through thinking man strives to solve the riddles of existence. Modern man is very proud of the naturalistic knowledge which, for three or four centuries, now, while marvelous relationships in nature were traced out, has been accumulating. But, precisely in regard to these relationships, presentday natural science must say to itself on reflection, with all intensity: What can be learned through the physical senses leads to a door which locks out world mysteries and cosmic riddles. And we know from anthroposophical contemplation that, to pass this door, to enter the realms where we may perceive what lies behind the outer world, we must overcome certain inner dangers. If a human being is to tread the path leading through this door, he must first attain, in his thoughts, feelings and will, a certain inner steadiness. That is why entering this door is called passing the Guardian of the Threshold. If real knowledge of the spiritual-divine foundation of the world is to be acquired, attention must be called not only to the dangers mentioned, but also to the fact that no person penetrates this door in the state of consciousness brought about between birth and death by merely natural conditions.

Here we should consider the tremendous seriousness of cognition. Also the abyss lying between the purely naturalistic world and the world we must seek if we would enter our true home and discover what bears a relationship to our inmost being. For in the merely naturalistic world we feel ourselves strangers in regard to this inmost being. On entering physical existence at birth, inevitably we carry with us our eternal-divine being; but if its source is to be recognized, we must first become aware of the abyss lying between earth life and the regions of cognition which we must enter in order to know our own being.

An understanding of cognition highlights, on the one hand, the gravity of the search for a true relationship with the spiritual world; on the other, it helps us to recognize that, if earthly existence were immediately satisfactory, if what modern naturalism dreams to be the case were so, namely, that man is merely the highest pinnacle of natural phenomena, there would exist no religious human beings. For in such circumstances man would have to be satisfied with earthly existence.

Religion aims at something entirely different. It presents a reality which reconciles man to earthly existence, or consoles him beyond earthly existence, or perhaps awakens him to the full meaning of earthly existence by making him aware that he is more than anything which earthly existence implies.

Thus the anthroposophical world-conception is capable of giving a strong impetus to cognition as well as to religious experience. In the case of cognition it stresses the fact that one must travel a road of purification before passing the gate to the spiritual world. On the other hand, it stresses the truth that religious life leads far beyond the facts observable by a person with only ordinary earthly consciousness. For Anthroposophy recognizes that the Mystery of Golgotha, the earth-life of Christ Jesus, though placed among historical events comprehensible to the senses, can be comprehended in its fulness only supersensibly.

Fortunately the abyss on the edge of which man lives, the abyss opening out before him in religion and cognition, can be bridged. But not by contemporary religion, nor yet by a cognition, a science, derived wholly from the earth.

It is here that art enters. It forms a bridge across the abyss. That is why art must realize that its task is to carry the spiritual-divine life into the earthly; to fashion the latter in such a way that its forms, colors, words, tones, act as a revelation of the world beyond. Whether art takes on an idealistic or realistic coloring is of no importance. What it needs is a relationship to the truly, not merely thought-out, spiritual. No artist could create in his medium if there were not alive in him impulses springing from the spiritual world. This fact points to the seriousness of art, standing alongside the seriousness of cognition and religious experience. It cannot be denied that our materialistically oriented civilization diverts us, in many ways, from the gravity of art. But any devoted study of true artistic creation reveals it as an earnest of man's struggle to harmonize the spiritual-divine with the physical-earthly.

This became evident at that moment of world-evolution when human beings were faced in all seriousness with the great question of art; became evident in the grand style during the time of Goethe and Schiller. A glance at their struggles will corroborate this statement. Much that is pertinent, here, has already been quoted in past years, in other connections. Today—to provide a basis for discussion—I shall cite only a few instances.

During the eighteenth century there emerged a guiding idea which Goethe and Schiller themselves accepted: namely, the differentiation between romantic and classical art. Espousing classicism, Goethe tried to become its nurturer by familiarizing himself with the secrets of great Greek art. His Italian journey was fulfilment of his longing. In Germany, that northern land, he felt no possibility of reconciling, artistically, the divine-spiritual hovering before his soul and the physical-sensory standing before his senses. Greek art, so abundant in Italy, and now deeply perceived, taught him the harmonization he lacked when he left Weimar for Italy. The impression he makes in describing his experience is—I must coin a paradoxical expression—at once heroic and touching.

In art Goethe was a classicist in the sense (if we use words which satisfactorily express his own idea) that he directed his gaze primarily toward the external, the sensory-real. But he was too profound a spirit not to feel a discrepancy between the sensory and that which derives from other realms, home of his soul. Sense-evidence should be purified, elevated through shaping, through an appropriate treatment. Thus Goethe the artist distilled from natural forms and human actions an element which, although presented imperfectly in the sensory-physical, could be brought to clarity without infidelity to the physical. In other words, he let the divine-spiritual shine through purified sensory forms. Always it was his earnest endeavor not to take up the spiritual lightly in his writings, not to express the divine-spiritual offhandedly. For he was convinced that romanticism can make only a facile, all-too-easy introduction of the spiritual into the physical; not deal with it comprehensively and effectively.

Never was it his intention to say: The gods live; I resort to symbolism to prove my conviction that the gods live. He did not feel thus. On the contrary, he felt somewhat as follows: I see the stones, I behold the plants, I observe the animals, I perceive the actions of human beings. To me all these creations have fallen away from the divine-spiritual. Nevertheless, though their earthly forms and colors show a desertion from the divine-spiritual, I must, by my treatment, lift them to a level where they can reflect, out of their own natures, that same divine-spiritual. I need not become unfaithful to nature—this Goethe felt—just purify seceded nature by artistic fashioning; then it will express the divine-spiritual. This was Goethe's conception of classicism; of the main impulse of Greek art, of all true art.

Schiller was unable to go along with this viewpoint. Because his gaze was directed idealistically into the spiritual world, he used physical things as indicators only. Thus he was the dayspring of post-Goethean romantic poetry. It is extraordinarily interesting to watch the reversal of method. For romantic poetry, as opposite pole to the classicism striven for by Goethe, despaired, as it were, of elevating the earthly-sensory to the divine; being satisfied to use it only as a more or less successful way of pointing to the divine-spiritual.

Let us look at the classicism of Goethe, composer of these beautiful lines:

> Who possesses science and art
> Possesses religion as well:
> Who possesses the first two not,
> O grant him religion.
> ("Wer Wissenschaft und Kunst besitzt,
> Hat auch Religion;
> Wer jene beiden nicht besitzt,
> Der habe Religion.")

Goethe, permeated by a conviction that every artist harbors the religious impulse, Goethe, to whom the trivially religious was repulsive because there lived in him a deep religious impulse, took the greatest pains to purify artistically the sensory-physical-earthly form to a point where it became an image of the divine-spiritual. Let us look at his careful way of working. He took up what was robustly earthly without feeling any necessity of changing it greatly to give it artistic form.

Consider, in this respect, his *Goetz von Berlichingen.* He treated the biography of this man objectively and with respect while dramatizing it, as demonstrated by the title of the first version: *Geschichte Gottfriedens von Berlichingen mit der eisernen Hand, dramatisiert* (*History of Gottfried of Berlichingen of the Iron Hand, Dramatized*). In other words, by changing only slightly the purely physical, he led it over into the dramatic; wishing, as artist, to part with the earth as little as possible; presenting it as a manifestation of the spiritual-divine world order.

Take another instance. Let us see how he approached his

Iphigenie, his *Tasso.* He conceived these dramas, shaped their subject matter, poetically. But what happened then? He did not dare to give them their final form. In the situation in which he found himself, he, Goethe, who was born in Frankfurt and studied in Leipzig and Strassburg before going to Weimar, he, the Weimar-Frankfurt Goethe, did not dare to finish these dramas. He had to go to Italy and walk in the light of Greek art to elevate the sensory-physical-earthly to a level where it could image forth the spiritual. Imagine the battle Goethe went through in order to bridge the abyss between the sensory-physical-earthly and divine-spiritual. It was like an illness when he left Weimar under cover of night, saying nothing to anybody, to flee to an environment in which he could master and elevate and spiritualize, as never in the north, the forms he worked with. His psychology is deeply moving. As I said before, it has about it something that might be called heroic-touching.

Let us go further. It is characteristic of Goethe—the paradox may strike you as peculiar—that he never finished anything. He began *Faust* in one great fling, but only the philistine Eckermann could induce him, in his old age, to bring this drama to a conclusion, and then it was only just barely possible for the author. For Goethe to bring his *Faust* to artistic form was a tremendous struggle which required the help of somebody else. Then take *Wilhelm Meister.* After its inception, he did not wish to finish. It was Schiller who persuaded him to do so. And if we scrutinize the matter, we might say: if only Schiller had not done so. For what Goethe then produced was not on the same level as his first sketch which would have remained a fragment. Take the second part: episodes are assembled. The writing is not all of a piece; it is not a uniform work of art. Now observe how—as in *Pandora*—Goethe strove to rise to the pinnacle of artistic creation by drawing his figures from the Greek world which he loved so much. *Pandora* remained a fragment, he could not complete it; the project was too vast for him to round it out. The serious, difficult task of the artist weighed upon his soul, and when he tried to idealize human life, to present it in the glory of the divine-spiritual, he could complete only the first part of the trilogy, the first drama: *Die Natuerliche Tochter.*

Thus in every possible way Goethe shows his predilection for the classical; always endeavoring, in his works, to purify the earthly physical to the point where it could spread abroad the radiance of the divine-spiritual. He struggled and strove, but the task was such that, apprehended deeply enough, it surpassed human forces, even Goethe's. We must say, therefore, that precisely in such a personality the arts with their grave world-mission appear in their full grandeur and power. What appeared, later, in romanticism is all the more characteristic when considered in the light of Goethe.

Last Thursday was the hundred-and-fifthieth birthday of Ludwig Tieck, who was born on May 31, 1773, and died on April 28, 1853. Tieck—unfortunately little known today—was in a certain respect a loyal pupil of Goethe. He grew out of romanticism, out of what at the University of Jena during the nineties of the eighteenth century was regarded as as the modern Goethe problem. In his youth he had experienced the publication of *Werther* and of the first part of *Faust.* At Jena, together with Novalis, Fichte, Schelling and Hegel, he struggled to solve the riddles of the world. In his immediate environment Ludwig Tieck felt the breath of Goethe's striving toward the classical, and in him we can see how spiritual life was still active at the end of the eighteenth, and during the first half of the nineteenth, century. With Schlegel, Tieck introduced Shakespeare into Germany; and as a personality he illustrates how Goethe's tremendous efforts were reflected in certain of his prominent contemporaries. Tieck felt the grandeur and dignity of art as a mighty cultural ideal. He looked about; he did not gather his life experiences in a narrowly circumscribed spot. After sitting at the feet of Fichte, Schelling and Hegel at the University of Jena, he journeyed through Italy and France. Then, after becoming acquainted with the world and philosophy, he strove, in a true Goethean manner, artistically to bridge the abyss between earthly and heavenly existence.

Of course he could not compete with Goethe's power and impetus. But let us look at one of Tieck's works: *Franz Sternbald's Wanderungen* (*Franz Sternbald's Journeys*), written in the form of *Wilhelm Meister.* What are these Sternbald journeys? They are journeys of the human soul into the realm of art. The question pressing heavily upon Sternbald is this: How can I raise sense-reality to the radiance of the spiritual? At the same time Tieck—whose hundred-and-fiftieth birthday we ought to be celebrating—felt the seriousness which streams down upon art from the region of cognition and that of religious life. Great is the light which falls, from there, upon Ludwig Tieck's artistic creations. A novel which he wrote comparatively early in life bears the title *William Lovell*; and this character is under Tieck's own impression (received while sitting at the feet of Schelling and Fichte in Jena) of the extreme seriousness of the search for knowledge. Imagine the effect of such teachings upon a spirit as receptive as Tieck's. (Differently, though not less magnificently, they influenced Novalis.) In his younger years Tieck had passed through the rationalistic "free spirit" training of Berlin's supreme philistine Nikolai. It was therefore an experience of the very greatest importance when he saw how in Fichte and Schelling the human soul relinquished, as it were, all connection with outer physical reality and, solely through its own power, endeavored to find a path through the door to the spiritual world. In *William Lovell* Tieck depicts a human being who, entirely out of the forces of his own soul, subjectively, seeks access to the spirit. Unable to find in the physical-sensory the divine for which Goethe constantly strove through his classical art, William Lovell seeks it nevertheless, relying entirely on his own forces, and thereby becoming confused, perplexed in regard to the world and his own personality. Thus William Lovell loses his hold on life through something sublime, that is, through the philosophy of Fichte and Schelling. In a peculiar way the book points out the dangers of cognition, through which, of necessity, men must pass. Tieck shows us how the cognitionally-serious can infuse the artistically-serious.

In his later years Ludwig Tieck created the poetic work: *Der Aufruhr in den Cevennen* (*The Uprising in the Cevennes*). What is his subject matter? Demonic powers which approach man, nature spirits which lay hold of him, possess him, drive him into religious fanaticism, and cause him to lose his way through the world. Oh, this Ludwig Tieck certainly felt what it means, on the one hand, to be dependent solely upon one's own personality and, on the other, to fall prey to elementals, gods of the elements. Hence overtones of gripping power in Tieck's works; for example in his *Dichterleben* (*Life of the Poet*) in which he describes how Shakespeare, as a thoroughly poetic nature, enters the world, how the world puts obstacles in his path, and how he stumbles into pitfalls. In *Dichterleben* Tieck discusses a poet's birth and all that earthly life gives him on a purely naturalistic basis. In *Tod des Dichters* (*Death of the Poet*) which deals with the last days of the Portuguese poet Camoens, he describes a poet's departure from life, his path to the gate of death. It is deeply moving how Tieck describes, out of the seriousness of the Goethe age, the beginning and end of an artist's life. What was great in Tieck was not his own personality, but rather his reflection of Goethe's spirit. Most characteristic, therefore, is his treatment of those "really practical people" who want to stand solidly on the earth without spiritual impulse in artistic presentation. Oh, there exists no more striking satire on novels about knights and robber barons than Tieck's *Blaubart* (*Bluebeard*). And, again, no more striking satire on the mawkishly emotional trying to be artistic than Tieck's *Der gestiefelte Kater* (*Puss-in-Boots*). The woeful excess of sentiment which mutters of the divine-spiritual (a sentimentality illustrated by the affected Iffland and babbling Kotzebue) he sends packing.

Ludwig Tieck reveals how the Goetheanism of the first half of the nineteenth century was mirrored in a receptive personality; how something like a memory of the great ancient periods played into the modern age; periods in which mankind, looking up to the divine-spiritual, strove to create, in the arts, memorials of the divine-spiritual. Such a personality represents the transition from an age still spiritually vital, at least in memory, to an age blinded by a brilliant natural-scientific world-conception and less brilliant life-practice; an age which will never find the spirit without the impetus which comes from direct spiritual perception, which is to say, from imagination, inspiration and intuition, as striven for by Anthroposophy.

Look, from this point of view, at the tremendous seriousness ensouling these writers. Not only Goethe but many others despaired of finding their way into the spiritual world through contemporary cultural life. Goethe did not rest until, in Italy, he had acquired an understanding of the way the Greeks penetrated the secrets of existence through their works of art. I have often quoted Goethe's statement: "It seems to me that, in creating their works of art, the

Greeks proceeded according to nature's own laws, which I am now tracing." Clearly, he believed that in their art the Greeks received from the gods something which enabled them to create higher works of nature, images of divine-spiritual existence. The followers of Goethe, still under his direct influence, felt compelled to return to ancient times, at least to ancient Greece, to attain to the spirit.

Herman Grimm, who in many ways still felt Goethe's living breath (I mentioned this in my last article in *Das Goetheanum*), said repeatedly that the ancient Romans resembled modern human beings; though they wore the toga, walked like moderns; whereas the ancient Greeks all seemed to have had the blood of the gods flowing through their veins. A beautiful, artistically felt statement! Indeed, it was only after the fifteenth century (I have often mentioned this) that man entered into materialism. It was necessary. We must not berate what the modern age brought. Had things stayed as they were, man would have remained deterministically dependent upon the divine spiritual world. If he was ever to become free, his passage into a purely material civilization was an historical necessity. In the book *Philosophy of Spiritual Activity* I have described modern man's attitude in this respect. But the evening glow of the ancient spiritual life was still lighting up the sky in Goethe's time, indeed, right up to the middle of the nineteenth century. Therefore his longing for Italy, his hope of finding there, through an echo from ancient Greece, something unattainable in his own civilization: the spirit. Goethe could not live without having seen Rome and a culture which, however antiquated, still enshrined the spiritual in the sensory-physical.

He was preceded in this mood by Johann Joachim Winckelmann, a kind of personification of that evening-glow of ancient spiritual life. Goethe's appreciation of Winckelmann comes out in his marvelously beautiful book on this man and his century: a glorious presentation of the strivings of a personality longing for the spirit. Through this book one senses what Goethe felt vividly: that Winckelmann went to the south, to Rome, to find in ancient spirituality the spirit he missed in the present and restore it. Winckelmann was intoxicated by his search for spirituality: Goethe could feel that. And his book is superb precisely because he was permeated with that same longing. In Rome both men sensed, at last, something of the breath of ancient spirituality. There Winckelmann traced the mysteries of art to remnants of Greek artistic impulses and absorbed them into his soul; there Goethe repeated the experience. Thus it was in Rome that Goethe rewrote *Iphigenie.* He had fled with his northern *Iphigenie* to Rome in order to rewrite it and give it the only form he could consider classical. Here he succeeded. Which cannot be said of the works written after he returned home.

In all this we see Goethe the artist's profoundly serious struggle for spirituality. Only after he had discovered in Raphael's colors and Michelangelo's forms the results of what he considered genuine artistic experience could his own search come to fruition. Thus he represents the evening glow of a spirituality lost and no longer valid for modern man.

Permit me, now, to make a personal remark. There was a certain moment when I felt deeply what Winckelmann said when he traveled south to discover the secrets of art, and how Goethe followed in his footsteps. At the same moment I could not but feel strongly that the time of our surrender to the evening glow had passed; we must now search with all our might for a new unfolding of spiritual life, must give up seeking for what is past. All this I experienced at the destiny-allotted moment when, years ago, I had to deliver some anthroposophical lectures about the evolution of world and man in the very rooms where Winckelmann lived during his Roman sojourn; the very rooms where he conceived his thoughts about Italian and Greek art, and enunciated the comprehensive ideas which filled Goethe with the enthusiasm expressed in his book on Winckelmann. Here in Winckelmann's quarters the conviction permeated me that something new must be stated on the path to spiritual life. A strange connection of destiny.

With this personal remark I conclude today's observations.

V

I SHOULD like to supplement last week's lectures on art. Often I had to emphasize that the spiritual evolution of mankind has proceeded from the unity of science, art and religion. In presentday spiritual life we have science, art and religion separated, yet can look back into the time when these three streams flowed from a common source. That source is seen most clearly if we go back four or five thousand years to poetry during the primeval ages; or, rather, to what would today be called poetry. To fathom the poetry of the bearers of ancient culture (it is nonsense, our looking for this culture in presentday primitive peoples) we must study the spiritual development of mankind in those ancient times through the Mysteries.

Let us examine the times when human beings did not look to the earth, but out into the cosmos to find a content for their spiritual life, or to satisfy the deepest needs of their souls. At that period those with clairvoyant faculties, seeing the fixed stars and movements of the planets, considered everything on earth a reflection of events taking place in its cosmic environment. We need only remind ourselves how the ancient Egyptians measured by the rising of Sirius the significance for their lives of the river Nile; how they considered the Nile's influence a result of what could be fathomed only by studying the relationship between stars out there in the cosmos. To the Egyptians their interplay in cosmic space was mirrored, on earth, by the activity of the Nile. This is but one example among many. For the conception held sway that occurrences in definite locations on earth imaged forth the observable mysteries of the starry heavens. We must also be clear about the fact that in ancient times human beings beheld in the heavens things quite different from those now being investigated and calculated with so-called astro-mechanics and astro-chemistry.

Today we shall direct our attention to the way people expressed themselves through poetry during the period when they received spiritual content for their souls in the manner described.

I refer to an age when all the arts, except poetry, were but little developed. The other arts existed, to be sure, but in only a rudimentary state because the human beings of that time were deeply conscious of the fact that with the word, created out of their organisms' innermost secret, they could express something supersensible, that language was fitted to express what appears in star-constellations and star-movements; far better fitted than the art-mediums using substances taken directly from the earth. For language originates in spiritual man—this they felt—and is therefore eminently adapted to what, from cosmic reaches, manifests here on earth. Poetry, then, was not an offspring merely of phantasy but of spiritual perception; and it was by this means that man learned what he in turn poured into the other arts. Poetry, which finds expression through words, was the medium by which man entered into soul-communion with the stars, the extra-earthly.

This soul-communion constituted the poetic mood. Through it man saw how thoughts not yet separated from objects gain pictorial expression in his vaultlike head, a head resembling the firmament; how thought represents a spiritual firmament, a celestial vault; how thought is inherent throughout the cosmos. Individual thoughts were expressed through the relative positions of the stars, by the way the planets moved past each other. In those ancient times man —unlike the free man of a later age—did not think merely by virtue of his own inner force. In every thought-movement he felt the after-image of some star-movement, in every thought-form the after-image of a constellation. Thus his thinking transported him into stellar space. The sunlight which illumined the day, and which would seem to be blinding out in the cosmos, was not considered the guide to wisdom, not the guiding force of thought, but, rather, sunlight as reflected by the moon. The following is ancient Mystery wisdom: During the day we see light with the physical body, at night we do more; we see it gathered up by the silver chalice of the moon. And this sunlight, collected by the moon, was regarded as the soul's Soma drink. Enspirited thereby, the soul could conceive those thoughts which were the result, the image, of the starry heavens.

Thus man as thinker felt as though the force of his thinking were located not in his earthly organism, but out where the stars were circling and forming constellations; he felt his soul poured out into the entire universe. If he had investigated combinations and separations of thoughts, he would have looked, not for laws of logic, but for the paths and constellations of the stars in the nightly firmament. The laws and images of his thinking existed in the heavens.

When he became aware of his feeling, it was not the abstract feeling of which we speak today in our abstract time, but rather the concrete feeling closely united with such inner experiences as that of breathing and blood circulation, the vital interweaving of the interior of the human body. Thus he felt himself existing not only upon the physical earth, but in planetary space. He did not say: In the human organism millions of blood corpuscles circle, but rather: Mercury and Mars are crossing Sun and Moon. To repeat: he felt his soul poured out into the universe; felt that, while with his thoughts he abode among the fixed stars and their constellations, with his feelings he lived within the sphere of the moving planets. Only with his will did he feel himself on earth. Considering the terrestrial an image of the cosmic he said to himself: When the forces of Jupiter, Moon, Venus and Sun strike the earth and penetrate its soil in the solid, liquid and aeroform elements, then from these elements will impulses penetrate into the human being, just as thought impulses penetrate into him from the fixed stars, and feeling impulses from planetary movements.

By such awareness, man could transplant himself into the time of the beginnings of primeval art. What is primeval art? It is nothing other than speech itself (a fact little understood today). For our speech is fettered to the material-earthly; it no longer manifests what it was when human beings, feeling transported into the Zodiac, incorporated into themselves from zodiacal constellations the twelve consonants, and from the movements of the planets past the fixed-star constellations, the vowels. At that time human beings did not intend to express through speech what they experienced upon earth, but rather what the soul experienced when it felt transported into the cosmos; which is why, in ancient times, speech flowered into poetry. The last remnants of such poetry are contained in the Vedas and, more abstractly, in the Edda. These are after-images of what, in greater glory, in much greater sublimity and majesty, had arisen directly out of the formation of languages during those ages when human beings could still feel their own soul life intimately united with cosmic movement and experience.

What is felt of all this in presentday poetry?

Poetry would not be poetry—and in our time much poetry is no longer poetry—if certain aspects of man's communion with the cosmos had not been kept. What remains is whatever in speech-formation passes beyond the prose meanings of words into rhythm, rhyme and imagination. For true poetry never consists of what is stated literally. Into the prose content of a poem, whether written down or, better, recited or declaimed, there must sound rhythm, beat, imagination. This points to elements not contained in prose; to a background which, in every true poetic work, cannot be understood but must be guessed at, divined. It is only the prose content which can be understood by the mind. The fact that poetry conveys something lying outside its words, for which the words are but a means, the fact that poetry's aura of mood echoes cosmic harmony, melody, imagination, this fact, even today, makes poetry poetry. We still can divine what it meant for Homer when he said: "Sing, oh Muse, the wrath of Achilles, son of Peleus." It was not the poet singing; it was the soul which has communion with cosmic movements singing *through* him. In the planets live the Muses. The epic Muse lives in one particular planet. It was into this planet that Homer felt transported: Sing, oh Muse, resound for me, celestial melody of the planets; relate the deeds of earthly heroes, Agamemnon, Achilles, Odysseus, Idomeneus, Menelaus; sing of how events appear, not from the limited standpoint of earth, but when the gaze is directed from stellar space. Could one ever believe that the magnificent, comprehensive images of the *Iliad* stemmed from a "frog-perspective"? No, they have not even air-perspective; they have star-perspective. For that reason, the *Iliad* story could not be told as though man had solely to do with man, for the gods influence actions; side by side with human agents, they perform their deeds. This is not frog-perspective, this is the stellar-perspective to which the soul of the poet longed to rise when he said: "Sing, oh Muse, the wrath of Achilles, son of Peleus."

From all this it can be clearly seen that the earthly medium which art—in the present case, poetry—makes use of is only a means to an end. The artistic element comes from treating the medium in such a way that the spiritual background, the spiritual worlds, may be divined; word, color, tone, form, being but pathways. If we wish to reawaken in mankind the true artistic mood, we must, to a certain degree, transport ourselves back into those ancient times when the celestial, the poetic mood, lived in the human soul. Then we will receive an impression of how best to use other media to carry art to the world of the spirit; which is what must happen if art wants to be art. Today our feeling has coarsened; we no longer sense what, in the not so distant past, has made art what it is.

For example, say that we see a mother carrying a little child: an elevating sight. We are familiar with the fact that the immediate form impression received therefrom is fixed only for a moment. The very next moment the mother's head position changes, the child in the mother's arms moves. What we have before us in the physical world is never still very long. Now let us look at Raphael's Sistine Madonna: the Mother and Child. Now, an hour from now, a year from now, it remains what it was; nothing has changed, neither child nor mother move. The moment has been fixed. That which in the physical world is still only a moment is here, so to speak, paralyzed. But it only seems so. Today we no longer feel what Raphael most certainly felt, asking, Am I allowed to do that? to fix with my brush a single moment? It is not a lie to convey an impression that the mother holds her child in the same manner today as yesterday? Is it right to impose upon anybody a prolongation of one particular moment? At present such a question appears paradoxical, even nonsensical. But Raphael asked it. And what answer arose in him? This artistic obligation:

You must atone in a spiritual way for your sin against reality, must lift the moment out of time and space, for within time and space it is a palpable untruth; must, through what you paint on the plane of your canvas, bestow eternity, arouse feelings which transcend the earthly plane.

This is what is called today, abstractly, Raphael's idealistic painting. His idealism is his justification for so unnaturally fixing the moment. What he invokes through the depths of his colors, through color harmony, he attains by precluding—spiritualizing—the third dimension. His use of colors elevates to the spiritual what is otherwise seen, materialistically, in the third dimension. Thus that which is not on but behind the plane through blue, not on but in front of the plane through red, that which steps out of the plane in a spiritual way (whereas the third dimension steps out of the plane only in a material way), bestows eternity on the moment. Which is precisely what must be bestowed upon the moment. Without the eternal, art is not art.

I have known people—artists, mainly—who hated Raphael. Why? Because they could not understand what is stated above; because they wanted to stop short with an imitation of what the moment presents but which, the next moment, is gone. Once I became acquainted with a Raphael hater who saw the greatest progress in his own painting in the fact that he was the first who had dared to stop sinning against nature; that is, had dared to paint all the hairy spots of the naked body really covered with hair. How inevitable that a man who considered this great progress should have become a Raphael hater. But the episode also shows how badly our time has forsaken the spirit-borne element in art, the element which knows why painting is based on the plane. Spatial perspective must be comprehended; it was necessary in our freedom-endowed fifth post-Atlantean period to learn to understand spatial perspective, that which conjures up on the plane not the pictorial, but the sculptural. The real thing, however, is color-perspective which overcomes the third dimension not by foreshortening and focusing, but by a soul-spiritual relationship between colors, say, between blue and red, or blue and yellow. Painting must acquire a color-perspective which overcomes space in a spiritual fashion. Thus can the artistic be brought back to what it was when it linked man directly to spiritual worlds.

At that time man felt the harmony between science, religion and art. This perception must again be aroused. An echo of it lived in Goethe; that was what made him so great. True, man in his freedom had to experience those three as separated: science, art, religion. But the division has made him lose the profundity of all three; above all, he has lost communion with the cosmos.

One need only exaggerate today's relation between art and science, between poetry and science. You may say I need not carry the problem to extremes to show the contemporary mis-relationship between poetry, art and science. But in a radical case the whole mis-relationship becomes clear. So I cite a radical case:

Once, in a certain city, there took place a meeting of scientists to discuss some great materialistic problems. You know the tremendous seriousness with which such meetings deal with scientific problems; a seriousness so great, no individual dares to approach it with his personality. He therefore places a lectern in front of him, lays his manuscript on it, and reads a paper; or rather, one scientist after another reads a paper. Personality is shoved aside. So strongly does this seriousness act, it is withdrawn from the individual and placed on the lectern; extremely serious! At such meetings every face looks grave. To be sure, they look like reflections of the lectern; but very serious indeed! At this particular meeting the chairman turned to a group of poets with the request that they create, out of their art, poems which could be launched, between courses, at the banquet to follow. Thus the gentlemen—perhaps there were also ladies—went from this serious meeting to a dinner party where poems were presented making fun, satirically, of the various sciences. You see the mis-relation between science and art. First the scientists dealt very seriously with the position of a June bug's mandible, or the chromosomes of a June bug's sperm; then, between meat and dessert, poems were read which satirized this very research. First the gentlemen went to extremes of seriousness, then laughed. There was no inner relationship. You might criticize my citing so extreme an example of our civilization. I cite it because it is characteristic, because it shows in a radical manner the presentday relationship between cognition and art, namely, no relationship at all. The gentlemen who made poems for the banquet understood nothing of the scientific papers. It is not quite possible to state the reverse, namely, that the worthy scientists did not understand the poems, although the poets assumed this, for they considered their work profound. But there is not much to be understood in such poetry and it may, therefore, be inferred that even the illustrious gathering understood it in some degree.

It is highly important for our time to observe how a homogeneous human spiritual life has been split into three parts which have fallen away from each other. For there is now a most urgent necessity to recompose the whole. If a philosopher speculates today about unity and doubleness, monism and dualism, he does so with a neutral mind, marshaling abstract concepts in defence of the one or the other. Both viewpoints can be proved equally well. In the ages whose relationship to art has just been sketched, a discussion of unity or duality, of the one with or without the other, aroused all the forces of men's soul. Whether the world sprang from an undivided source, or whether, on the contrary, good and evil are two divided original powers, the battle between monism and dualism was in bygone ages an artistic-religious concern which aroused all the forces of the human soul, and upon which man felt that his welfare, his bliss, depended. Though in former times he considered these questions closely bound up with his salvation, today he speaks of them with indifference. If we do not acquire a breath of the artistic-religious-cognitional soul mood which once held sway, there will be no impulse toward the truly great in art.

Still another feeling lived in those ages. People spoke of the Soma drink, of sunlight poured into the silver moon-chalice, the reality with which they filled their souls in order to understand the secrets of the cosmos. Speaking of the Soma drink, they felt themselves in direct soul communion with the cosmos. Soul experiences took place simultaneously on earth and in the cosmos. People felt that the gods revealed themselves through fixed stars and orbiting planets. By forming images of themselves on earth, the fixed star constellations and planetary movements made it possible for the soul to experience a cosmic element. If it drank the Soma drink and carried out sacrifices in a ritualistic-artistic-cognitional manner, the soul gave back to the gods, in the rising smoke to which it entrusted the religious-artistic-poetic, word, what the gods needed for continued world creation. For the gods did not create man in vain; he exists on earth in order that something which can be achieved only by man may be used by the gods for further world creation. Man is on earth because the gods need him. He is on earth so that he may think, feel and will what lives in the cosmos. If he does it in the right way, the gods can take this changed thing and implant it into the configuration of the world.

Thus man—if in sacrifice and art he gives back what the gods gave him—cooperates in building the cosmos. He has a soul-connection with cosmic evolution.

If we permeate ourselves with a conception of this relationship within spiritual-physical cosmic evolution, we can apply it to the present world. There we see a cognition which wishes only to fashion matter, and which applies earthly laws and calculations even to astro-chemistry and astronomy; a cognition—the so-called scientific one—which holds good only for earth evolution. But this cognition will cease to be of significance to the degree that the earth is transformed into Jupiter, Venus, Vulcan. To repeat: today "science" has only an earthly meaning; its purpose is to help human beings to become free here on earth; but the gods cannot use this science for the continued cosmic creation.

Abstract thoughts are the ultimate abstraction, the corpse of the spirit world. What is carried out scientifically has meaning only for the earth. Having acted on earth as thought, it is shattered, buried; it does not live on.

In truth, what Ursula Karin, grandmother of the poet Adalbert Stifter, told him about the sunset glow belongs more intensively to the cosmos than what is to be read today in scientific books. Take everything in those books about the way sunlight acts on clouds to produce the evening glow, collect everything described there as natural laws: it has an earthly significance only. The gods cannot gather it up from earth to use it in the cosmos. Adalbert Stifter's grandmother said to the boy: "Child, what is the evening glow? Child, when it appears, the Mother of God is hanging out her clothes; she has so many to hang out on the heavenly dome."

This is an utterance on which the gods can draw for the further development of the world. Modern science tries to describe in precise concepts what exists now. But this will never become future; it is of the present. But Adalbert Stifter's grandmother, having preserved much of what lived in ancient souls, said something about which a modern scientist could only smile. He might consider it beautiful, but would have no inkling of the fact that her words are of greater significance for the cosmos than all his vaunted science. From whatever is useful in this sense, from whatever creates not space-and-time thoughts but eternally-active thoughts, all true art has arisen. Just as the imagination of Adalbert Stifter's grandmother, which made him a poet, is related to a dry materialistic conception, so Raphael's Sistine Madonna, which transcends the moment, which seizes the moment for the eternal, is related to any mother with her child seen here on the physical earth.

This is what I wished to add to our previous considerations, hoping to deepen them.

VI

TODAY I would like to examine certain other aspects of our subject.

I have often dealt with the genius of language, and you know from my book *Theosophy* that we refer to real spiritual entities when we speak of spiritual beings in an anthroposophical context. Thus "genius of language" designates the spiritual entity behind any specific language, an entity with whom man can become familiar and through whom he can receive, from the spiritual world, strength to express his thoughts which, at the outset, are present in his earthly self as a dead heritage from that higher world. It is, therefore, appropriate for anthroposophical students to seek, in the formation of language, a meaning which is independent of man because rooted in the spirit.

I have already drawn attention to the peculiar way the German language designates the beautiful and its opposite. We speak of the opposite of the beautiful (*das Sckoene*) as the ugly or hateful (*das Haessliche*). Were we to denote the beautiful in the same way we would call it—since the opposite of hate is love—the lovely or loving. As it is, we make a significant difference. In German the word beautiful (*das Schoene*) is related to shining (*das Scheinende*). The beautiful shines; brings its inner nature to the surface. It is the distinguishing quality of the beautiful not to hide itself, but to carry its essence into outer configuration. Thus beauty reveals inwardness through outer form; a shining radiates outward into the world. If we were to speak, in this sense, of beauty's opposite, we would call it the concealed or non-radiant, that which holds back its being, refusing to disclose it in any outer sheath. To put it another way, "the beautiful" designates something objective. If we were to treat its opposite just as objectively, we would have to speak of concealment, of something whose outer aspect belies what it really is. But here subjectivity enters, for we cannot love what conceals itself, showing a false countenance; we must hate it. In this way the ugly calls up quite a different emotional reaction than the beautiful; we do not respond to it out of the same recesses of our nature.

Thus the genius of language reveals itself. And we should ask: When in the broadest sense we strive for the beautiful in art, what is our goal? The very fact that the German word for "beautiful" proceeds outward (as its opposite suggests a remaining within our emotions, our hate) means that the beautiful bears a relation to the spiritual outside us. For what shines? What we apprehend with our senses does not need to shine for us; it exists. It is the spiritual that shines, radiating into the sensory, proclaiming its being even in the sensory. By speaking objectively of the beautiful, we take hold of it as a spiritual element which reveals itself in the world through art. The task of art is to take hold of the shining, the radiance, the manifestation, of that which as spirit weaves and lives throughout the world. All genuine art seeks the spirit. Even when art wishes to represent the ugly, the disagreeable, it is concerned, not with the sensory-disagreeable as such, but with the spiritual which proclaims its nature in the midst of unpleasantness. If the spiritual shines through the ugly, even the ugly becomes beautiful. In art it is upon a relation to the spiritual that beauty depends.

Proceeding from this truth, let us consider one of the

arts: painting. Recently we dealt with it insofar as it reveals the spiritual-essential through shining color. In ancient times man, by surrendering in the right way to the genius of language, showed his inner knowledge of color in his vocabulary. When an instinctive clairvoyance prevailed, he felt that metals revealed their inner natures in their colors, therefore gave them, not earthly names, but names connecting them with the planets. Otherwise people would have felt ashamed. For man looked upon color as a divine-spiritual element bestowed upon earthly substances only in the sense of our recent lectures. Perceiving the gold in gold's color, he saw not merely the earthly in that metal but the sun proclaiming itself from the cosmos in its gold color. Indeed, from the very start man saw something transcending the earthly in the colors of earthly objects. But it was only to living things that particular colors were ascribed, for living things approach the spirit in such a way that the spiritual shines forth. Animals were felt to have their own colors because in them the spirit-soul element manifests directly.

In ancient times, when man's artistic sense was not outward but inward, he painted not at all. To paint a tree green is not true painting for the reason that however well one imitates her, nature is still the essential thing; nature is still more beautiful, more vital; it needs no copy. A real painter never imitates. He uses an object as a recipient or focus of the sun, or to observe a color reflex in that object's surroundings, or to catch, above it, an interweaving of light and darkness. In other words, the thing painted is merely an inducement. For example, we never paint a flower standing in front of a window; we paint the light which, shining in at the window, is seen *through* the flower. We paint the sun's colored light; catch the sun.

In the case of a person, this can be done still more spiritually. To paint a human forehead the way one believes it should look is nonsense; this is not painting. But to observe how the sun rays strike that forehead, how color shows up in the ensuing radiance, how light and darkness intermingle, to capture with one's paint brush all that interplay: this is the task of the painter. Seizing what passes in a moment, he relates it to the spiritual.

If, with a sense for painting, we look at an interior view, the matter of most importance is not the figure or figures therein. I once accompanied a friend to an exhibition where we saw a painting of a man kneeling before an altar, his back toward us. The painter had given himself the task of showing how sunlight falling through a window struck the man's back. My friend remarked that he would much rather see a front view. Well, this was only material, not artistic, interest. He wanted the painter to show the man's character, and so forth. But one is justified in doing this only if one expresses all perceptions through color. If I wish to paint a human being sick in bed with a certain disease, and study his facial color in order to apprehend how illness shines through the sensory, this may be artistic. If I want to show, in totality, the extent to which the whole cosmos manifests in the human flesh color, this may also be artistic. But if I try to imitate Mr. Lehman as he sits here before me, I will not succeed; moreover, this is not the task of art. What is artistic is how the sun illumines him, how light is deflected through his bushy eyebrows. Thus for a painter the important thing is how the whole world acts upon his subject; and his means of holding fast to a transitory moment are light and darkness, the whole spectrum.

In times not so long ago one could not imagine a presentation of Mary, the Mother of God, without a face so transfigured it had passed beyond the ordinary human state; a face overcome by light. One could not imagine her clothed otherwise than in a red garment and blue cloak, because only so is the Mother of God placed rightly into earthly life; the red garment depicting all the emotions of the earthly, the blue cloak the soul element which weaves the spiritual around her; the face permeated and transfigured by spirit, overcome by light as a revelation of the spirit. We do not, however, properly and artistically take hold of these truths if we stop with what I have just described. For I have translated the artistic into the inartistic. We feel them artistically only if we create directly out of red and blue and the light by experiencing the light, in its relationship to colors and darkness, *as a world in itself*. Then colors speak their own language, and the Virgin Mary is created out of them.

To achieve this one must live with color; color must become emancipated from the heavy matter opposing its innermost nature. Palette colors are alien to true painting in that, when used on a plane surface, they have a down-dragging effect. One cannot live with oil-based colors, only with fluid colors. When a painter puts fluid colors upon a plane, color—owing to the peculiar relationship between man and color—springs to life; he conceives out of color; a world arises out of it. True painting comes into being only if he captures the shining, revealing, radiating element as something living; only if he creates what is to be formed on the plane out of this element. For to understand color is to understand a component part of the world.

Kant once said: Give me matter, and out of it I shall create a world. Well, you could have given him matter endlessly without his ever being able to make a world out of it. But out of the interplaying medium of color a world of sorts can indeed be created, because every color has direct relationship with something spiritual. In the face of presentday materialism, the concept and activity of painting have—except for the beginnings made by impressionism and, still more, by expressionism—been more or less lost.

For the most part modern man does not paint, he imitates figures with a kind of drawing, then colors the surface. But colored surfaces are not painting for the reason that they are not born out of color and light and darkness.

We must not misunderstand things. If somebody goes wild and just lays on colors side by side in the belief that this is what I call "overcoming drawing," he is mistaken. By "overcoming drawing" I do not mean to do away with drawing, but to let it rise out of the colors, be born from the colors. Colors will yield the drawing; one simply has to know how to live in colors. Living so, an artist develops an ability—while disregarding the rest of the world—to bring forth works of art out of color itself.

Look at Titian's "Ascension of Mary." This painting stands at the boundary line of the ancient principle of art. The living experience of color one finds in Raphael and, more especially, in Leonardo da Vinci has departed; only a certain tradition prevents the painter from totally forsaking the living-in-color.

Experience this "Ascension of Mary." The green, the red, the blue, cry out. Now take the details, the individual colors and their harmonious interaction, and you will feel how Titian lived in the element of color and how, in this instance, he really created out of it all three worlds.

Look at the wonderful build-up of those worlds. Below, he has created out of color the Apostles experiencing the event of Mary's ascension. One sees in the colors how these men are anchored to the earth; colors which convey, not heaviness in the lower part of the painting, only a darkness which fetters the watching ones to earth. In the color-treatment of Mary one experiences the intermediate realm. A dull darkness from below connects her feet and legs with the earth; while, above her, light preponderates. This third and highest realm receives her head and radiates above it in full light, lifting it up. Thus are set forth, through inner color experience, the three stages of lower realm, middle realm, and the heights where Mary is being received by God the Father.

To understand this picture we must forget everything else and look at it solely from the standpoint of color, for here the three stages of the world are derived from color not intellectually but artistically. True painting takes hold of this world of effulgent shining, of splendid manifestation in light and darkness and color, in order to contrast what is earthly-material with the artistic. But the artistic is not permitted to reach the spiritual. Otherwise it would be not "shine" but wisdom. For wisdom is no longer artistic, wisdom leads into the formless and therefore undepictable realm of the divine.

With artistry like Titian's in "The Ascension of Mary," we feel, on beholding the reception of Mary's head by God the Father, that now we must go no further in the treatment of light; we must halt. For we have reached the limit of the possible. To carry it further would be to fall into the intellectualistic, the inartistic. We must not make one stroke beyond what is indicated by light, rather than contour. The moment we insist on contour, we become intellectualistic, inartistic. Near the top this picture is in danger of becoming inartistic. The painters immediately after Titian fell prey to this danger. Look at the depiction of angels right up to the time of Titian. They are painted in heavenly regions. But look how carefully the painters avoided leaving the realm of color. Always you can ask yourself in regard to these angels of the pre-Titian age, and of Titian too: Couldn't they be clouds? If you cannot do that, if there is no uncertainty about existence, being, or semblance, shine, if there is an attempt fully to delineate the essence of the spiritual, artistry ceases.

In the seventeenth century it was otherwise, for materialism affects the presentation of the spiritual. Now angels began to be painted with all kinds of foreshortenings, and one can no longer ask: Couldn't that be clouds? When reason is active, artistry dies.

Again, look at the Apostles below: one has a feeling that in this "Ascension of Mary" only Mary is really artistic. Above, there is the danger of passing into the formlessness of pure wisdom. If one attains the formless one attains, in a certain sense, the zenith of the artistic. One has dared to press forward boldly to the abyss where art ceases, where the colors disappear in light, and where, if one were to proceed, one could only draw. But drawing is not painting. Thus the upper part of the picture approaches the realm of wisdom. And the more one is able to express, in the sensory world, this wisdom-filled realm, and the more the angels might be taken for billowy clouds shimmering in light, the greater the art.

Proceeding from the bottom of the picture to the really beautiful, to Mary herself rising into the realm of wisdom, we see that Titian was able to paint her beautifully because she has not yet arrived at, but only soars up toward, the realm of wisdom; and we feel that, were she to rise still higher, she must enter where art ceases. Below stand the Apostles. Here the artist has tried to express their earth-fettered character. But now a different danger threatens. Had he placed Mary further down, he could not have depicted her inward beauty. If Mary were to sit among the Apostles, she could not appear as she does as a kind of balance between heaven and earth; she would look different. She simply does not fit among the Apostles with their brownish tones. Not only are they subject to earthly gravity; something else has entered: the element of drawing takes hold. This you can see in Titian's picture. Why is it so?

Well, brown having already left the realm of color, it cannot express Mary's beauty; something not belonging entirely to the realm of the beautiful would be injected. If Mary stood or sat among the Apostles and were colored as they are, it would be a great offense. I am now speaking only of this picture and do not maintain that when standing on earth Mary must be in every instance, artistically speaking, an offense. But in this picture it would be a blow in the face if Mary stood below. Why?

Because if she stood there colored like the Apostles we would have to say that the artist presented her as virtuous. This is the way he presents the Apostles; we cannot conceive of them otherwise than looking upward in their virtue. But this for Mary would be inappropriate. With her, virtue is so self-evident that we must not express it. It would be like presenting God as virtuous. If something is self-evident, if it has become the being itself, we must not express it in mere outer semblance. Therefore Mary soars up into a region beyond all virtues, where we cannot say of her, through colors, that she is virtuous, any more than we can say of God that He is virtuous. He may, at most, be virtue itself. But this is an abstract, philosophical statement having nothing to do with art. With the Apostles, however, the artist succeeded in representing, through his color treatment, virtuous human beings. They are virtuous.

Let us look at how the genius of language reflects this truth. *Tugend* (virtue, in German) is related to *taugen* (to be fit, in German). To be fit, to be able to cope with something morally, is to be virtuous. Goethe speaks of a triad: wisdom, semblance and power. Art is the middle term: semblance, the beautiful; wisdom is formless knowledge; virtue is power to carry out worthwhile things effectively.*

Since ancient times this triad has been revered. Once, years ago, a man said to me—and I could appreciate his point of view—that he was sick and tired of hearing people speak of the true, the beautiful and the good, for anyone in search of an idealistic expression mouthed the phrase. But in ancient times these realities were experienced not externally but with complete soul participation. Thus in the upper region of Titian's picture we see wisdom not yet transcendent, radiating artistically because of the way it is painted. In the middle, beauty; below, virtue, that which is fit. What is the inner nature of the fit? Here is manifest the genius, the profundity, of the languages active among men. If we proceeded in an exterior way we might be reminded of a certain hunchback who went to church and listened to a priest describing quite externally how everything in the world is good and beautiful and fit. Waiting at the church door, the hunchback asked the priest: You said the idea of everything is good—have I, too, a good shape? The priest replied: For a hunchback you have a very good shape.

If things are considered as externally as this, we shall never penetrate to the depths. In many fields modern observation proceeds so. Filled with external characteristics and definitions, men do not know that their ideas turn round and round in circles.

In respect to virtue it is not a question of fitness for just anything, but of fitness for something spiritual, so that a person places himself into the spiritual world as a human being. Whoever is a complete human being by reason of his bringing the spiritual not merely to manifestation but to full realization through his will is—in the true sense—virtu-

* The English word virtue, derived from the Latin *vir,* man, carries a similar connotation of power. (Translators)

ous. Here we enter a region which lies within the human and religious, but no longer within the artistic, sphere, and least of all within the sphere of the beautiful. Everything in the world contains a polarity. Thus we can say of Titian's picture: Above Mary he is in danger of passing beyond the beautiful, there where he reaches the abyss of wisdom. Below, he comes to the brink of the other abyss. For as soon as a painter represents the virtuous, meaning that which man realizes through his own being, out of the spiritual, he again leaves behind the beautiful, the artistic. The virtuous human being can be painted only by characterizing virtue in its outer appearance, let us say by contrasting it with vice. But an artistic presentation of virtue as such is no longer possible.

Where in our age do we not forsake the artistic? Simple life conditions are reproduced crudely, naturalistically, without any relation to the spiritual, and without this relation there is no art. Hence the striving of impressionism and expressionism to return to the spiritual. Though in many cases clumsy, tentative, exploratory, it is better than the inartistic copying of a model.

Furthermore, if one grasps the concept of the artistically-beautiful, one can deal with the tragic in its artistic manifestations. The human being who acts in accordance with his thoughts, who lives his life intellectualistically, can never become really tragic. Nor can the human being who leads an entirely virtuous life. The only tragic person is one who in some way leans toward the daimonic, that is to say, toward the spiritual, whether in a good or bad sense. Today in this age when man is in the process of becoming free, daimonic man, that is man under the influence of tutelary spirits, is an anachronism. That man should outgrow the daimonic and become free is the whole meaning of the fifth post-Atlantean age. But as he progresses in freedom the possibility of tragedy diminishes and finally ceases. Take ancient tragic characters, even most of Shakespeare's: they have a daimonism which leads to the tragic. Wherever man had the appearance of the daimonic-spiritual, wherever the daimonic-spiritual radiated and manifested through him, wherever he became its medium, tragedy was possible. In this sense the tragic will have to taper off now; a free mankind must rid itself of tutelary spirits. This it has not yet done. On the contrary, it is more and more falling prey to such forces.

But the great task and mission of the age is to pull human beings away from the daimonic towards freedom. The irony is that the more we get rid of the inner daimons which make us tragic personalities, the less do we get rid of external ones. For the moment modern man enters into relation with the outer world, he encounters something of the nature of daimons. Our thoughts must become freer and freer. And if, as I say in *The Philosophy of Spiritual Activity,* thoughts become will impulses, then the will also becomes free. These are polaric contrasts in freedom: free thoughts, free will.

Between lies that part of human nature which is connected with karma. And just as once upon a time the daimonic led to tragedy, so now the experiencing of karma can lead to inmost tragedy. Tragedy will flourish when man experiences karma. As long as we live in our thoughts we are free. But the words with which we have clothed our thoughts, once spoken or written, no longer belong to us. What may happen to a word I have uttered! Having absorbed it, somebody else surrounds it with different emotions and sensations, and thus the word lives on. As it flies through the world it becomes a power proceeding from man himself. This is his karma. Because it connects him with the earth, it may burst in on him again. Even the word which leads its own existence because it belongs not to us but to the genius of language may create the tragic. Just in our present time we see mankind at the inception of tragic situations through an overestimation of language, of the word. Peoples wish to separate themselves according to language, and their desire provides the basis for the gigantic tragedy which during this very century will break in upon the earth. This is the tragedy of karma. If past tragedy is that of daimonology, future tragedy will be that of karma.

Art is eternal; its forms change. And if in everything artistic there is some relationship to the spiritual, you will understand that with the artistic we place ourselves, creatively or through enjoyment, in the spirit world. A real artist may create his picture in a lonely desert. He does not worry about who will look at his picture or whether anybody at all will look at it, for he creates within a divine-spiritual community. Gods look over his shoulder; he creates in their company. What does he care whether or not anybody admires his picture. A person may be an artist in complete loneliness. Yet he cannot become one without bringing, by means of his creation, something spiritual into the world, so that it lives in the spirituality of the world. If one forgets this basic connection, art becomes non-art.

To create artistically is possible only if the work has a relationship to the world. Those ancient artists who painted pictures on the walls of churches were conscious of this fact; they knew that their murals stood within earth life insofar as this is permeated by the spirit; that they guided believers.

One can hardly imagine anything worse than painting for exhibitions. It is horrible to walk through a picture or sculpture gallery where completely unrelated subjects appear side by side. Painting lost meaning when it passed from something for church or home to an isolated phenomenon. If we paint or view a picture in a frame, we can imagine ourselves looking out through a window. But to paint for exhibitions—this is beyond discussion. An age which sees value in exhibitions has lost its connection with art. By this can be seen how much waits to be done in culture if we would find our way back to the spiritual-artistic. Exhibitions must be overcome. Of course some individual artists detest exhibitions. But today we live in an age when the individual cannot achieve very much unless his judgment grows out of a world-conception permeating fully free human beings; just as world-conceptions permeating people in less free ages led to the rise of genuine cultures. Today we have no real culture.

Only a spiritual world-conception can build up true culture, the indubitably artistic.

VII

WE MUST emphasize again and again that the anthroposophical world-conception fosters a consciousness of the common source of art, religion and science. During ancient periods of evolution these three were not separated; they existed in unity. The Mysteries which fostered that unity were a kind of combination art institute, church and school. For what they offered was not a one-sided sole dependence upon language. The words uttered by the initiate as both cognition and spiritual revelation were supported and illustrated by sacred rituals unfolding, before listening spectators, in mighty pictures.

Thus alongside the enunciation of earthly knowledge, religious rituals imaged forth what could be divined and perceived as events and facts of the supersensible worlds. Religion and cognition were one. Moreover, the beautiful, the artistic, had its place within the Mysteries · ritual and image, acting together, produced a high art. In other terms, the religiously-oriented rituals which fired man's will and the knowledge-bearing words which illumined him inwardly had, both, a strong ally in the beautiful, the artistic. Thus consciousness of the brotherly unity of religion, science and art must today be ever-present in anthroposophical world-research; an interlinkage brought about not artificially, but in a self-evident, natural way.

Modern intellectualistic-materialistic science tries to grasp the world in thoughts. As a result, certain ideas give conceptual form to the phenomena of nature and its creatures. We translate natural laws into thoughts. During the recent materialistic age it was characteristic of those preoccupied with cognition that they gradually lost artistic sensibility. Acceptance of modern science means yielding to dead thoughts and looking for them in nature. Natural history, that proud achievement of our science, consists of dead thoughts, corpses of what constituted our soul before we descended from supersensible into sensory existence.

Anyone looking at the corpse of a human being can see by his form that he could not have achieved this state through any mere laws of nature as we know them; he had first to die. A living person became a corpse by dying. Similarly anyone with real cognition knows that his thoughts are corpses of that vital soul-being within which he lived before incarnation. Our earth-thoughts are actually corpses of our pre-earthly soul-life. And they are abstract precisely because they are corpses. As people during the last few centuries became more and more enamored of abstractions, of these thoughts which insinuated themselves into practical life, they came more and more to resemble them in their higher soul-life. Especially people with a scientific education. This estranged them from art. The more one surrenders to purely abstract thoughts, dead thoughts, the more one becomes a stranger to art. For art desires and is centered on the living.

A soul seriously occupied with anthroposophical cognition enters the opposite state. Whereas intellectuality approaches everything from the standpoint of logic, and tries to explain even the arts according to logical rules, in anthroposophical thinking there arises at a certain moment a great longing for art. For this different type of cognition leads to a realization that thoughts are not the whole living reality; something else is needed. Since the entire soul life now remains living instead of being killed by dead thoughts, one comes to need to experience the world artistically. For if one lives in abstract dead thoughts, art is only a luxury formed out of man's dreams and illusions; an addition to life. But—to repeat—the anthroposophical method of knowledge brings one to a realization that thoughts are not the living reality; they are dead gestures which merely point to that reality; and at a certain stage one feels that, to attain reality, one must begin to create; must pass over to art. Ideas alone simply cannot present the world in its rich full content. Thus Anthroposophy prepares the soul for artistic feeling and creating.

Abstract thoughts deaden artistic phantasy. Becoming more and more logical, one takes to writing commentaries on works of art. This is a terrible product of a materialistic age: scholars write commentaries on art. But these academic explanations, *Faust* commentaries, *Hamlet* commentaries, learned descriptions of the art of Leonardo, Raphael, Michelangelo, are coffins in which genuine artistic feeling, living art, lie buried. If one picks up a *Faust* or *Hamlet* commentary, it is like touching a corpse. Abstract thoughts have murdered the work of art.

Anthroposophy, on the other hand, tries to approach art out of the living spirit—as I did in speaking of Goethe's *Fairy Tale of the Green Snake and the Beautiful Lily.* I did not write a commentary, I let the living lead me into the living. During an inartistic age there appear many scholarly treatises on art, works on aesthetics. They are non-art, counter-art. Savants may reply: To take hold of the world artistically is to move away from reality; it is not scientific; if reality is to be seized, phantasy has to be suppressed, imagination eliminated; one must confine oneself to the logical. This may be demanded. But consider: If reality, if nature herself were an artist, then it would be of no avail to demand that everything be grasped solely through logic; something vital in it would elude logical understanding. And nature is indeed an artist; a truth discovered by anthroposophical cognition at a certain point in its development. Therefore, in order to grasp nature, especially the highest in nature, man's physical form, one must cease to live exclusively in ideas and begin to "think" in pictures. No anatomy, no physiology, can ever grasp the physical human being in his forms. Understanding is achieved only by living cognition that has been given wings by artistic feeling.

Thus it was inevitable that the idea to build a Goetheanum flowed over into artistic creation. Anthroposophical ideas flowered into artistic forms. The same ideas manifested in a different manner. This is the way true art always develops in the world. Goethe who was able to feel artistically has coined the following beautiful words: "Art is a manifestation of secret laws of nature which, without it, would remain forever hidden." He felt what anthroposophists must feel. If one has attained to a cognitional comprehension of the world, there arises a vital need not just to continue forming ideas but to create artistically in sculpture, painting, music, poetry.

But then an unfortunate thing may happen. If one tries, as I tried in my four Mystery dramas, to present what cannot be expressed in ideas concerning the essential nature of man, there spring up sympathetic but not fully comprehending people who try to explain everything in ideas, who write commentaries. This—I repeat—is an appalling thing. It happens because the deadening element of abstract thought is often carried even into the anthroposophical movement. Actually, within this movement there should be a continual quickening of abstract thoughts. What can no longer be experienced intellectually can be enjoyed through living dramatic characters as they move before and confront us. Beholding them we let them act upon us as real figures instead of trying to explain them abstractly. Genuine Anthroposophy leads, inevitably, at a certain point, into art because, far from thought-killing, it inspires us; permits the artistic spring in the human soul to gush forth.

Then one is not tempted to form ideas symbolically or allegorically, but to let all ideas flow to a certain point and to follow the purely artistic form. Thus the Goetheanum architecture rose completely idea-less (if I may use that odd expression) as a result of feeling the forms out of the spirit. It should be seen, not explained. When I had the honor of conducting guests through the Goetheanum, I usually made introductory remarks something like this: "You naturally expect me to explain the building, but this is uncongenial. During the next half hour, while guiding you, I must do something I very much dislike, for the Goetheanum is here to be seen, not explained." This I emphasized over and over, for the edifice standing there should live as image, not in abstract deadening thoughts. Explanations being unavoidable, I tried to make mine not abstract but imbued with the feelings embodied in the building's own forms, pictures, colors. One can be spiritual in forms, colors, tones, as well as words. Indeed, only then does one experience the really artistic. For here in our sense world art is always an influx of the supersensible. We can perceive this truth in any work of art which presents itself in forms having their origin in human nature.

Take the art of architecture which, to a large degree, today serves utilitarian purposes. To understand architectural forms, one must feel the human form itself artistically. This is necessarily accompanied by a feeling that man has forsaken the spiritual worlds to which he rightfully belongs. A bear in its fur or a dog in its pelt shows itself well cared for by the universe; one senses a totality. If, on the other hand, one looks artistically at man, one realizes that, seen merely from the viewpoint of the senses, he lacks something. He has not received from the universe what the well-coated bear and dog received. In sense appearance he stands, as it were, naked to the world. The need is to see, by means of a purely artistic approach, man's physical body clothed by an imaginative-spiritual sheath.

Today, in architecture, this reality does not manifest clearly. But take the pinnacle reached by architecture when it created protective covers for the dead. As noted earlier, the monuments erected above graves at the starting point of architecture had great meaning. Primeval instinctive clairvoyance perceived that, after forsaking its physical body, its earthly prison, the naked soul shrinks from being released into cosmic space without first being enveloped by those forms by which it wants to be received. People held that the soul must not simply be turned loose into the chaotically interacting weather currents; they would tear it apart. The soul desires to expand into the universe through regular spatial forms. For this reason it must be surrounded by tomb-architecture. It cannot find its bearings in the storms of weather and wind which rush toward it; only in the artistic forms of the monument above the grave. Here paths into the cosmic reaches are formed. An enveloping sheath such as man, unlike plants and animals, never receives through sensory-natural elements, is given the soul out of the supersensible.

Thus one can say: Originally architecture expressed the manner in which man wants to be received by the cosmos. In a house the forms should be similarly artistic. The planes, the lines: why are they there? Because the soul wishes to look out into space in those directions, and to be protected from inrushing light. If one considers the relation of the soul to the spatial universe, if one recognizes how that universe welcomes the soul of man, one arrives at the right architectural forms.

Fine architecture has a counterpart. When man leaves his physical body at death, his soul spreads into spatial forms. Architecture strives to reveal this relation of man to visible cosmic space. At birth he possesses an unconscious memory of his own pre-earthly existence. Modern man's consciousness retains nothing of this. But in unconscious feeling, especially when naively artistic, the down-plunging soul knows that previously it was quite different. And now it does not wish to be as it finds itself on dipping down into the body. It longs to be as it was before.

This desire shows up in primitive people. Because they feel artistically how they would prefer to live in their body, they first decorate and then clothe themselves, the colors of their garments displaying how they would—while in the body—present their souls. Corporeality does not suffice them, through color they would place themselves in the world in a way that harmonizes with what they feel themselves as souls. Whoever views with artistic sense the colorful clothes of primitive people sees a manifestation of the soul in space; and in like manner, in architectural forms, the disappearing of the soul into space. Here we have the impulses at work in two arts: architecture and costuming.

This art of costuming merges with the other arts. It is not without meaning that in ages with more artistic feeling than ours, say the Italian Renaissance, painters gave Mary Magdalene a color of gown different from that of Mary. Compare the yellow so often used in the robes of Mary Magdalene with the blue and red in those of Mary, and you see the soul-difference perceived by a painter living wholly in his medium.

We who love to dress grey in grey simply show the world the deceased image of our soul. In our age we not only think abstractly, we dress abstractly. And (this is said parenthetically) if we do not dress abstractly, then we show in the way we combine colors how little we retain the living thinking of the realms through which we passed before descending to earth. If we do not dress abstractly, we dress without taste. In our civilization it is precisely the artistic element that needs improvement. Man must again place himself vitally-artistically into the world; must perceive the whole cosmic being and life artistically. It will not suffice to use the well-known apparatus of research institutes for determining the angle of a face and measuring abstractly racial peculiarities; we must recognize the form through a sensitive *qualitative* immersion in the human being.

Then in a marvelous way we shall recognize in the human head, in its arching of forehead and crown, a copy—not just as allegory but inward reality—of the heavenly dome dynamically overarching us. An image of the universe is shaped by forehead and upper head. Similarly, an image of our experience in circling the sun, in turning round it with our planet in a horizontal circling, this participation in cosmic movement is felt artistically in the formation of nose and eyes. Imagine: the repose of the fixed stars shows in the tranquil vault of brow and upper head; planetary circling in the mobile gaze of the eye, and in what is inwardly experienced through nose and smell. As for the mouth and chin of man, we have here an image of what leads deeply into his inner nature. The mouth with the chin represents the whole human being as he lives with his soul in his body. To repeat, the human head mirrors the universe artistically. In forehead and the arching crown of the head we see the still vault of the heavens; in eye, nose and upper lip, planetary movement; in mouth and chin, a resting within oneself.

If all this is beheld as living image, it does not remain in the head as abstraction. If we really feel what I have just described, then a certain sensation arises and we say to ourselves: you were quite a clever man who had pretty ideas, but now, suddenly, your head becomes empty; you cannot think at all; you feel the true significance of forehead, crown, eye, nose, upper lip, mouth, lower lip, even while thoughts forsake you. Now the rest of man becomes active. Arms and fingers begin to act as tools of thinking. But thoughts live in forms. It is thus that a sculptor comes into being.

If a person would become a sculptor, his head must cease to think. It is the most dreadful thing for a sculptor to think with his head. It is nonsense; impossible. The head must be able to rest, to remain empty; arms and hands must begin to shape the world in images. Especially if the human image is to be recreated, the form must stream out of the fingers. Then one begins to understand why the Greeks with their splendid artistry formed the upper part of Athene's head by raising a helmet which is actually part of that head. Her helmet gives expression to the shaping force of the reposing universe. And one understands how, in the extraordinary shaping of the nose, in the way the nose joins the forehead in Greek profiles, in the whole structure, the Greeks expressed a participation in circling cosmic motion.

Oh, it is glorious to feel, in the artistic presentation of a Greek head, how the Greeks became sculptors. It is thus a spiritual sensing and beholding of the world, rather than cerebral thinking, which leads to art, and which receives an impulse from Anthroposophy. For the latter says to itself: There is something in the world which cannot be tackled by thought; to enter it at all you must start to become an artist. Then materialistic-intellectualistic scholarship appears like a man who walks around things externally and describes them logically, but still only skirts them from outside, whereas the anthroposophical way of thinking demands that he immerse himself in the not-himself, and recreate, with living formative force, what the cosmos created first.

Thus gradually one realizes the following: If as anthroposophist you acquire a real understanding of the physical body which falls away from cosmic space-forms to become a corpse, if you acquire an understanding of the way the soul wishes to be received by spatial forms after death, you become an architect. If you understand the soul's intention of placing itself into space with the unconscious memories of pre-earthly life, then you become an artist of costuming: the other pole from the architectural.

One becomes a sculptor if one feels one's way livingly into the human form as it is shaped by and emerges from the cosmos. If one understands the physical body in all its aspects one becomes, artistically, an architect. If one really grasps the etheric or formative-force body (as it is called in Anthroposophy) in its inner vitality, in its living and weaving, in the way it arches the forehead, models the nose, lets the mouth recede, one becomes a sculptor. The sculptor does nothing more nor less than imitate the form of the etheric body.

If now one looks at soul-life in all its weaving and living, then the manifold world of color becomes a universe; then one gradually acquaints oneself with an "astral" experience of the world. What manifests in color becomes a revelation of the realm of soul.

Let us look at the greenness of plants. We cannot consider this color a subjective experience, cannot think of vibrations as causing the colors, the way a physicist does, for if we do so we lose the plant. These are abstractions. In truth we cannot imagine the plants in a living way without the green. The plant produces the green out of itself. But how? Embedded in it are dead earth-substances thoroughly enlivened. In the plant are iron, carbon, silicic acid, all kinds of earth-substances found, also, in minerals. But in the plant they are woven through and through with life. In observing how life works its way through dead particles to create thereby the plant image, we recognize green as the dead image of life. Everywhere that we look into green surroundings we perceive, not life itself, but its image. In other words, we perceive plants through the fact that they contain dead substances; this is why they are green. That color is the dead image of life ruling on earth. Green is thus a kind of cosmic word proclaiming how life weaves and has its being in plants.

Now look at man. The color which comes closest to a healthy human flesh color is that of fresh peach blossoms in spring. No other color in nature so resembles this skin color, this flush. The inner health of man comes to expression in this peach-blossom-like color; and in it we can learn to apprehend the vital health of man when properly endowed by soul. If the flesh color tends toward green, he is sickly; his soul cannot find right access to his physical body. On the other hand, if the soul in egotistical fashion takes hold of the physical body too strongly, as in the case of a miser, the human being becomes pallid, whitish; also if the soul experiences fear. Between whitish and greenish tones lies the healthy vital peach-blossom flesh-tint. And just as we sense in green the dead image of life, so we can feel in the peach-blossom color of the healthy human being the living image of the soul.

Now the world of color comes to life. The living, through the dead, creates the picture green. The soul forms its own image on the human skin in the peach-blossom-like shade.

Let us look further. The sun appears whitish, and we feel that this whitish color is closely related to light. If we wake in pitch darkness, we know that this is not an environment in which we can fully experience our ego. For that we need light between us and objects; need light between us and the wall, for instance, to allow the wall to act on us from the distance. Then our sense of self is kindled. To repeat: if we wake in light, in what has a relation to white, we feel our ego; if we wake in darkness, in what is related to black, we feel strange in the world. Though I say "light," I could just as well take another sense impression. You may find a certain contradiction because those born blind never see light. But the important matter is not whether or not we see light directly; it is how we are organized. Even if born blind, man is organized for the light, and the hindrance to ego energy present in the blind is so through absence of light. White is akin to light. If we experience light-resembling white in such a way that we feel how it kindles the ego in space by endowing it with inner strength, then we may express living, not abstract, thought by saying: White is the soul-appearance of spirit.

Now let us take black. When our spirit encounters darkness on waking, we feel paralyzed, deadened. Black is felt as the spiritual image of death.

Imagine living in colors. You experience the world as color and light if you experience green as the dead image of life; peach-blossom color, human flesh-color, as the living image of the soul; white as the soul-image of spirit; black as the spiritual image of death. In saying this I describe a circle. For just note what I said: Green, dead image of the living—it stops at "living." Peach-blossom color, flesh-color, living image of the soul—It stops at "soul." White, soul-image of the spirit—having started with soul I rise to the spirit. Black, spiritual image of death—I start with spirit and rise to death; but have at the same time returned, since green was the *dead* image of life. Returning to what is dead I close the circle. If I drew it on a blackboard you would see that this living weaving in color (in the next lecture I shall speak of blue) becomes a real artistic experience of the astral element in the world.

If one has this artistic experience, if death, life, soul and spirit show forth, as it were, in the wheel of life as one passes from the dead back to the dead through life, soul, spirit; if death, life, soul and spirit appear through light and color as described, then one realizes that one cannot remain in three-dimensional space, one must adopt the plane surface; solve the riddle of space on the plane; lose the space concept.

Just, as sculptors, we abandoned head thinking, so now we lose the concept of space. When everything wants to change into light and color we become painters. The very source of painting opens up. With great inner joy we lay one color alongside another. Colors become revelations of life, death, soul, spirit. By overcoming dead thought we attain to the point where we no longer feel impelled to speak in words, no longer to think in ideas, no longer to mould in forms, but use color and light to represent life and death, spirit and soul, as they have their being in the universe.

In this way Anthroposophy stimulates creation; instead of weaning us away from life as does abstract, idealistic-empirical cognition, it gives us back to life.

But so far we have remained outside man, considering his surface: his healthy peach-blossom tones, his pale-whitish color when his spirit plunges too deeply into the physical body, and his greenish shade when, because of sickness, his soul cannot fill that body. We have remained on the surface.

If we now enter man's inner nature, we find something set against the external world-configuration: a marvelous harmony between the breath rhythm and blood rhythm. The rhythm of breathing—a normal human being breathes eighteen times per minute—is transferred to man's nerves, becomes motion. Physiology knows very little about this process. The rhythm of breathing is contained, in a delicate psycho-spiritual manner, in the nerve system.

As for the blood rhythm, it originates in the metabolic

system. In a normal adult, four pulse beats correspond to one breath rhythm; seventy-two pulse beats per minute. What lives in the blood, that is, the ego, the sunlike nature in man, plays upon the breathing system and, through it, upon the nervous system. If one looks into the human eye, one finds there some extremely fine ramifications of blood vessels. Here the blood pulsation meets the currents of the visual nerve spread through the eye. A marvelously artistic process takes place when the blood circulation plays upon a visual nerve that moves four times more slowly.

Now look at the spinal cord, its nerves extending in all directions, observe the blood vessels, and become aware of an inward playing of the whole sun-implanted blood system upon the earth-given nervous system. The Greeks with their artistic natures were aware of this interrelation. They saw the sun-like in man, the playing of the blood system upon the nervous system, as the God Apollo; and the spinal cord with its wonderful ramification of strings, upon which the sun principle plays, as Apollo's lyre.

Just as we meet architecture, sculpture, the art of costuming and painting when we approach man from the external world, so we meet music, rhythm, beat, when we approach the inner man and trace the marvelous artistic forming and stirring which take place between blood and nerve system.

Compared to external music, that performed between blood and nerve system in the human organism is of far greater sublimity. And when it is metamorphosed into poetry, one can feel how, in the word, this inward music is again released outward. Take the Greek hexameter with its initial three long syllables followed by a caesura, and how the blood places the four syllable lengths into the breath. To scan the first half of an hexameter line properly is to indicate how our blood meets, impinges on, the nervous system.

In relation to declamation and recitation, we must try to solve the riddle of the divine artist in man. I shall consider this more explicitly in the next lecture. But, having studied man's nature from without through architecture, sculpture and painting, we now penetrate into his inner nature and arrive at the arts of music and poetry; a living comprehension of world and man passes over into artistic feeling and the stimulus to artistic creation.

If at this point man feels that here on earth he does not fulfil what lies in his archetype, with its abode in the heavens, then there arises in him an artistic longing for some outer image of that archetype. Whereupon he can gain the power to become an instrument for bringing to expression the true relation of man to the world by becoming a eurythmist. The eurythmist says: All the movements which I ordinarily carry out here on earth do less then justice to the mobile archetype of man. To present the ideal human archetype I must begin by finding a way to insert myself into its motions. These motions, through which man endeavors to imitate in space the movements of his heavenly archetype, constitute eurythmy. Therefore it is not just mimicry, nor mere dancing, but stands midway between. Mimic art is chiefly a support for the spoken word. If the need is to express something for which words do not suffice, man supplements word with gesture; thus arises mimic art. It expresses the insufficiency of the words standing alone. Mimic art is indicative gesture.

The art of dancing arises when language is forgotten altogether, when the will manifests so strongly it forces the soul to surrender and follow the movement-suggesting body. The art of the dance is sweeping ecstatic gesture.

We may say: mimic art is indicative gesture; art of dance, sweeping ecstatic gesture. Between the two stands the visible speech of eurythmy which is neither indicative nor sweeping but *expressive* gesture, just as the word itself is expressive gesture. For a word is really a gesture in air. When we form a word, our mouth presses the air into a certain invisible gesture, imbued with thought, which, by causing vibrations, becomes audible. Whoever is able with sensory-supersensory vision to observe what is formed by the speaking mouth sees, in air, the invisible gestures being made there as words. If one imitates these gestures with the whole body, one has eurythmy, an expressive *visible* gesture. Eurythmy is the transformation of an air gesture into a visible expressive gesture of the limbs.

I shall touch on all this in my coming lecture on Anthroposophy and poetry. Today I wished chiefly to indicate how anthroposophical, in contrast to intellectualistic-materialistic, knowledge does not kill with its thoughts; does not turn a person into a commentator on art who thereby buries it, but, rather, causes an artistic spring, a fountain of phantasy, to well up. Turns him into an enjoyer or creator of art; verifies what must be emphasized over and over again, namely, that art, religion and science are sisters who once upon a time became estranged, but who must again enter into a sisterly relationship if man is to function as a complete human being. Thus scholars will cease haughtily to acknowledge a work of art only if they can write a commentary on it and otherwise reject it, but will say: What I interpret as thought engenders a need to fashion it artistically by means of architecture, sculpture, painting, music, poetry.

Goethe's saying that art is a kind of knowledge is true, because all other forms of knowledge, taken together, do not constitute a complete world knowledge. Art—creativity—must be added to what is known abstractly if we are to attain to world knowledge. This union of art and science will produce a religious mood. Because our Dornach building strove for this balance, friends of nationalities other than German petitioned to call it the "Goetheanum," for it was Goethe who said:

Who possesses science and art
Possesses religion as well;
Who possesses the first two not,
O grant him religion.

For if true art and true science flow together livingly, the result is a religious life. Conversely religion, far from denying science or art, must strive toward both with all possible energy and vitality.

VIII

DAY before yesterday I tried to show that the anthroposophical knowledge which accompanies an inner life of the soul does not estrange one from artistic awareness and creation. On the contrary, whoever takes hold of Anthroposophy with full vitality opens up within himself the very source of such activity. And I indicated how the meaning of any art is best read through its own particular medium.

After discussing architecture, the art of costuming, and sculpture, I went on to explain the experience of color in painting, and took pains to show that color is not merely something which covers the surface of things and beings, but radiates out from them, revealing their inner nature.

For instance, I pointed out that green is the image of life, revealing the life of the plant world. Though it has its origin in the plant's dead mineral components, it is yet the means whereby the living shows forth in a dead image. It is fascinating that life can thus reveal itself. In that connection, consider how the living human figure appears in the dead image of sculpture; how life can be expressed through dead, rigid forms. In green we have a similar case in that it appears as the dead image of life without laying claim to life itself.

I shall repeat still other details from the last lecture in order to show how the course of the world moves on, then returns into itself; and shall do this by presenting the colors which make up its various elements: life, soul, spirit. I said I would draw this complete circle of the cosmic in the world of color. As I told you before, green appears as the dead image of life; in green life lies, as it were, concealed.

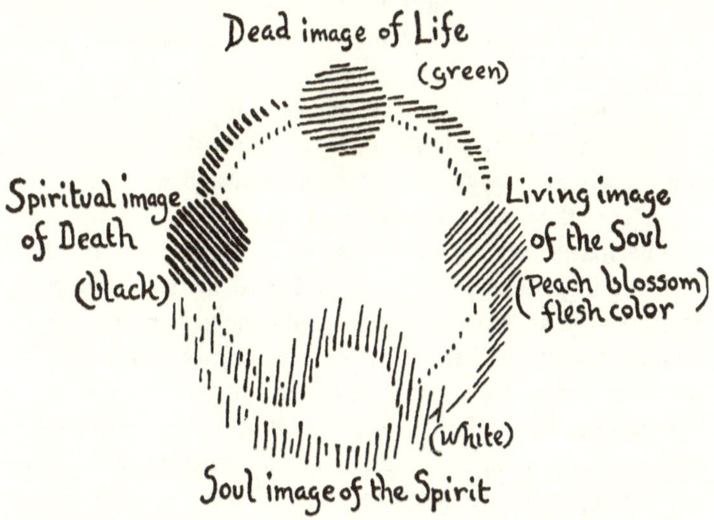

If we take the flesh color of Caucasian man, which resembles spring's fresh peach-blossom color, we have the living image of the soul. If we contemplate white in an artistic way, we have the soul image of the spirit. (The spirit as such conceals itself.) And if, as artists, we take hold of black, we have the spiritual image of death. And the circle is closed.

I have apprehended green, flesh color, white and black in their aesthetic manifestation; they represent the self-contained life of the cosmos within the world of color. If, artistically, we focus attention upon this closed circle of colors, our feeling will tell us of the need to use each of them as a self-contained image.

Naturally, in dealing with the arts I must concern myself not with abstract intellect, but aesthetic feeling. The arts must be recognized artistically. For that reason I cannot furnish conceptual proof that green, peach-blossom, white and black should be treated as self-contained images. But it is as if each wants to have a contour within which to express itself. Thus they have, in a sense, shadow natures. White, as dimmed light, is the gentlest shadow; black the heaviest. Green and peach-blossom are images in the sense of saturated surfaces; which makes them, also, shadowlike. Thus these four colors are image or shadow colors, and we must try to experience them as such.

The matter is quite different with red, yellow and blue. Considering these colors with unbiased artistic feeling, we feel no urge to see them with well-defined contours on the plane, only to let them radiate. Red shines toward us, the dimness of blue has a tranquil effect, the brilliance of yellow sparkles outward. Thus we may call flesh color, green, black and white the image or shadow colors, whereas blue, yellow and red are radiance or lustre colors. To put it another way: In the radiance, lustre and activity of red we behold the element of the vital, the living; we may call it the lustre of life. If the spirit does not wish merely to reveal itself in abstract uniformity as white, but to speak to us with such inward intensity that our soul can receive it, then it sparkles in yellow; yellow is the radiance or lustre of the spirit. If the soul wishes to experience itself inwardly and deeply, withdrawing from external phenomena and resting within itself, this may be expressed artistically in the mild shining of blue, the lustre of the soul. To repeat: red is the lustre of life, blue the lustre of the soul, yellow the lustre of the spirit.

Colors form a world in themselves and we understand them with our feelings if we experience the lustre colors red, yellow, blue, as bestowing a gleam of revelation upon the image colors, peach-blossom, green, black and white. Indeed, we become painters through a soul experience of the world of color, through learning to live with the colors, feeling what each individual color tries to convey. When we paint with blue we feel satisfied only if we paint it darker at the edge and lighter toward the center. If we let yellow speak its own language, we make it strong in the center and gradually fading and lightening toward the periphery. By demanding this treatment, each reveals its character. Thus forms arise out of the colors themselves; and it is out of their world that we learn to paint sensitively.

If we wish to represent a spiritually radiant figure, we cannot do otherwise than paint it a yellow which decreases in strength toward its edge. If we wish to depict the feeling soul, we can express this reality with a blue garment—a blue which becomes gradually lighter toward its center. From this point of view one can appreciate the painters of the Renaissance, Raphael, Michelangelo, even Leonardo, for they still had this color experience.

In the paintings of earlier periods one finds the inner or color-perspective of which the Renaissance still had an echo. Whoever feels the radiance of red sees how it leaps forward, how it brings its reality close, whereas blue retreats into the distance. When we employ red and blue we paint in color-perspective; red brings subjects near, blue makes them retreat. Such color-perspective lives in the realm of soul and spirit.

During the age of materialism there arose spatial perspective, which takes into account sizes in space. Now distant things were painted not blue but small; close things not red but large. This perspective belongs to the materialistic age which, living in space and matter, prefers to paint in those elements.

Today we live in an age when we must find our way back to the true nature of painting. The plane surface is a vital part of the painter's media. Above everything else, an artist, any artist, must develop a feeling for his media. It must be so strong that—for instance—a sculptor working in wood knows that human eyes must be dug out of it; he focuses on what is concave; hollows out the wood. On the other hand, a sculptor working in marble or some other hard substance does not hollow out; he focuses his attention on, say, the brow jutting forward above the eye; takes into consideration what is convex. Already in his preparatory work in plasticine or clay he immerses himself in his material. The sculptor in marble lays on; the woodcarver takes away, hollows out. They must live with their material; must listen and understand its vital language.

The same is true of color. The painter feels the plane surface only if the third spatial dimension has been extinguished; and it is extinguished if he feels the qualitative character of color as contributing another kind of third dimension, blue retreating, red approaching. Then matter is abolished instead of—as in spatial perspective—imitated. Certainly I do not speak against the latter. In the age which started with the fifteenth century it was natural and self-evident, and added an important element to the ancient art of painting. But today it is essential to realize that, having passed through materialism, it is time for painting to return to a more spiritual conception, to return to color-perspective.

In discussing any art we must not theorize but (I repeat) abide, feelingly, within its own particular medium. In speaking about mathematics, mechanics, physics, we must kill our feeling and use only intellect. In art, however, real perception does not come by way of intellect, art historians of the nineteenth century notwithstanding. Once a Munich artist told me how he and his friends, in their youth, went to a lecture of a famous art historian to find out whether or not they could learn something from him. They did not go a second time, but coined an ironical derogatory phrase for all his theorizing. What can be expressed through the vital weaving of colors can also be expressed through the living weaving of tones. But the world of tones has to do with man's inner life (whereas the sculptor in three-dimensional space and the painter on a two-dimensional plane express what manifests etherically in space). With the musical element we enter man's inner world, and it is extremely important to focus attention upon its meaning within the evolution of mankind.

Those of my listeners who have frequently attended my lectures or are acquainted with anthroposophical literature know that we can go back in the evolution of mankind to what we call the Atlantean epoch when the human race, here on earth, was very different from today, being endowed with an instinctive clairvoyance which made it possible to behold, in waking dreams, the spiritual behind the physical. Parallel to this clairvoyance man had a special experience of music. In those ancient days music gave him a feeling of being lifted out of the body. Though it may seem paradoxical, the people of those primeval ages particularly enjoyed the chords of the seventh. They played music and sang in the interval of the seventh which is not today considered highly musical. It transported them from the human into the divine world.

During the transition from the experience of the seventh to that of the pentatonic scales, this sense of the divine gradually diminished. Even so, in perceiving and emphasizing the fifth, a feeling of liberating the divine from the physical lingered on. But whereas with the seventh man felt himself completely removed into the spiritual world, with the fifth he reached up to the very limits of his physical body; felt his spiritual nature at the boundary of his skin, so to speak, a sensation foreign to modern ordinary consciousness.

The age which followed the one just described—you know this from the history of music—was that of the third, the major and minor third. Whereas formerly music had been experienced outside man in a kind of ecstasy, now it was brought completely within him. The major and minor third, and with them the major and minor scales, took music right into man. As the age of the fifth passed over into that of the third man began to experience music inwardly, within his bounding skin.

We see a parallel transition: on the one hand, in painting the spatial perspective which penetrates into space; on the other, in music, the scales of the third which penetrate into man's etheric-physical body; which is to say, in both directions a tendency toward naturalistic conception. In spatial perspective we have external naturalism, in the musical experience of the third "internal" naturalism.

To grasp the essential nature of things is to understand man's position in the cosmos. The future development of music will be toward spiritualization, and involve a recognition of the special character of the individual tone. Today we relate the individual tone to harmony or melody in order that, together with other tones, it may reveal the mystery of music. In the future we will no longer recognize the individual tone solely in relation to other tones, which is to say according to its planal dimension, but apprehend it in depth; penetrate into it and discover therein its affinity for hidden neighboring tones. And we will learn to feel the following: If we immerse ourselves in the tone it reveals three, five or more tones; the single tone expands into a melody and harmony leading straight into the world of spirit. Some modern musicians have made beginnings in this experience of the individual tone in its dimension of depth; in modern musicianship there is a longing for comprehension of the tone in its spiritual profundity, and a wish—in this as in the other arts—to pass from the naturalistic to the spiritual element.

Man's special relationship to the world as expressed through the arts becomes clear if we advance from those of the outer world, that is architecture, art of costuming, sculpture and painting, to those of the inner world, that is to music and poetry. I deeply regret the impossibility of carrying out my original intention of having Frau Dr. Steiner illustrate, with declamation and recitation, my discussion of the poetic art. Unfortunately she has not yet recovered from a severe cold. During this Norwegian lecture course my own cold forces me to a rather inartistic croaking, and we did not want to add Frau Dr. Steiner's.

Rising to poetry, we feel ourselves confronted by a great enigma. Poetry originates in phantasy, a thing usually taken as synonymous with the unreal, the non-existent, with which men fool themselves. But what power expresses itself through phantasy?

To understand that power, let us look at childhood. The age of childhood does not yet show the characteristics of phantasy. At best it has dreams. Free creative phantasy does not yet live and manifest in the child. It is not, however, something which, at a certain age in manhood, suddenly appears out of nothingness. Phantasy lies hidden in the child; he is actually full of it. What does it do in him? Whoever can observe the development of man with the unbiased eye of the spirit sees how at a tender age the brain, and indeed the whole of his organism, is still, as compared with man's later shape, quite unformed. In the shaping of his own organism the child is inwardly the most significant sculptor. No mature sculptor is able to create such marvelous cosmic forms as does the child when, between birth and the change of teeth, it plastically elaborates his organism. The child is a superb sculptor whose plastic power works as an inner formative force of growth. The child is also a musical artist, for he tunes his nerve strands in a distinctly musical fashion. To repeat: power of phantasy is power to grow and harmonize the organism.

When the child has reached the time of the change of teeth, around his seventh year, then advances to puberty, he no longer needs such a great amount of plastic-musical power of growth and formation as, once, for the care of the body. Something remains over. The soul is able to withdraw a certain energy for other purposes, and this is the power of phantasy: the natural power of growth metamorphosed into a soul force. If you wish to understand phantasy, study the living force in plant forms, and in the marvelous inner configuratons of the organism as created by the ego; study everything creative in the wide universe, everything molding and fashioning and growing in the subsconscious regions of the cosmos; then you will have a conception of what remains over when man has advanced to a point in the elaborating of his own organism when he no longer needs the full quota of his power of growth and formative force. Part of it now rises up into the soul to become the power of phantasy. The final left-over (I cannot call it sediment, because sediment lies below while this rises upward)—the ultimate left-over is power of intellect. Intellect is the finely sifted-out power of phantasy, the last upward-rising remainder.

People ignore this fact. They see intellect as of greater reality. But phantasy is the first child of the natural formative and growth forces; and because it cannot emerge as long as there is active growing, does not express direct reality. Only when reality has been taken care of does phantasy make its appearance in the soul. In quality and essential nature it is the same as the power of growth. In other words, what promotes growth of an arm in childhood is the same force which works in us later, in soul transformation, as poetic, artistic phantasy. This fact cannot be grasped theoretically; we must grasp it with feeling and will. Only then will we be able to experience the appropriate reverence for phantasy, and under certain circumstances the appropriate humor; in brief, to feel phantasy as a divine, active power in the world.

Coming to expression through man, it was a primary experience for those human beings of ancient times of whom I spoke in the last lecture, when art and knowledge were a unity, when knowledge was acquired through artistic rites rather than the abstractions of laboratory and clinic; when physicians gained their knowledge of man not from the dissecting room but from the Mysteries where the secrets of health and disease, the secrets of the nature of man, were divulged in high ceremonies.

It was sensed that the god who lives and weaves in the plastic and musical formative forces of the growing child continues to live in phantasy. At that time, when people felt the deep inner relationship between religion, art and science, they realized that they had to find their way to the divine, and take it into themselves for poetic creation; otherwise phantasy would be desecrated.

Thus ancient poetic drama never presented common man, for the reason that mankind's ancient dramatic phantasy would have considered it absurd to let ordinary human beings converse and carry out all kinds of gestures on the stage. Such a fact may sound paradoxical today, but the anthroposophical researcher—knowing all the objections of his opponents—must nevertheless state the truth. The Greeks prior to Sophocles and Aeschylus would have asked: Why present something on the stage which exists, anyhow, in life? We need only to walk on the street or enter a room to see human beings conversing and gesturing. This we see everywhere. Why present it on a stage? To do so would have seemed foolish.

Actors were to represent the god in man, and above all the god who, rising out of terrestrial depths, gave man his will power. With a certain justification our predecessors, the ancient Greeks, experienced this will-endowment as rising up out of the earth. The gods of the depths who, entering man, endow him with will, these Dionysiac gods were to be given stage presentation. Man was, so to speak, the vessel of the Dionysiac godhead. Actors in the Mysteries were human beings who received into themselves a god. It was he who filled them with enthusiasm.

On the other hand, man who rose to the goddess of the heights (male gods were recognized as below, female gods in the heights), man who rose in order that the divine could sink into him became an epic poet who wished not to speak himself but to let the godhead speak through him. He offered himself as bearer to the goddess of the heights that she, through him, might look upon earth events, upon the deeds of Achilles, Agamemnon, Odysseus and Ajax. Ancient epic poets did not care to express the opinions of such heroes; opinions to be heard every day in the market place. It was what the goddess had to say about the earthly-human element when people surrendered to her influence that was worth expression in epic poetry. "Sing, oh goddess, the wrath of Achilles, son of Peleus": thus did Homer begin the *Iliad*. "Sing, oh goddess, of that ingenious hero," begins the *Odyssey*. This is no phrase; it is a deeply inward confusion of a true epic poet who lets the goddess speak through him instead of speaking himself, who receives the divine into his phantasy, that child of the cosmic forces of growth, so that the divine may speak about world events.

After the times had become more and more materialistic, Klopstock, who still had real artistic feeling, wrote his *Messiade*. Inasmuch as man no longer looked up to the gods, he did not dare to say: Sing, oh goddess, the redemption of sinful man as fulfilled here on earth by the Messiah. He no longer dared to do this in the eighteenth century, but cried instead: "Sing, oh immortal soul, of sinful man's redemption." In other words, he still possessed something which was lifted above the human level. His words reveal a certain bashfulness about what was fully valid in ancient times: "Sing, oh goddess, the wrath of Achilles, son of Peleus."

Thus the dramatist felt as if the god of the depths had risen, and that he himself was to be that god's vessel; the epic poet as if the Muse, the goddess, had descended into him in order to judge earthly conditions. The ancient Greek actor avoided presentation of the individual human element. That is why he wore high thick-soled shoes, *cothurni,* and used a simple musical instrument through which his voice resounded. He desired to lift the dramatic action above the individual-personal.

I do not speak against naturalism. For a certain age it was right and inevitable. For when Shakespeare conceived his dramatic characters in their supreme perfection, man had arrived at presenting, humanly, the human element. Quite a different urge and artistic feeling held sway at that period. But the time has come when, in poetic art also, we must find our way back to the spiritual, to presenting dramatic figures in whom man himself, as a spiritual as well as bodily being, can move within the all-permeating spiritual events of the world.

I have made a first weak attempt in my Mystery dramas. There human beings converse not as people do in the market place or on the street, but as they do when higher spiritual impulses play between them, and their instincts, desires and passion are crossed by paths of destiny, of karma, active through millennia in repeated lives.

It is imperative to turn to the spiritual in all spheres. We must make good use of what naturalism has brought us; must not lose what we have acquired by having for centuries now held up, as an ideal of art, the imitation of nature. Those who deride materialism are bad artists, bad scientists. Materialism had to happen. We must not look down mockingly on earthly man and the material world. We must have the will to penetrate into this material world spiritually; nor despise the gifts of scientific materialism and naturalistic art; must—though not by developing dry symbolism or allegory—find our way back to the spiritual. Symbolism and allegory are inartistic. The starting point for a new life of art can come only by direct stimulation from the source whence spring all anthroposophical ideas. We must become artists, not symbolists or allegorists, by rising, through spiritual knowledge, more and more into the spiritual world.

It can be attained quite specially if, in the art of recitation and declamation, we transcend naturalism. In this connection we should remember how genuine artists like Schiller and Goethe formed their poems. In Schiller's soul there lived an indefinite melody, and in Goethe's an indefinite picture, a form, before ever they put down the words of their poems. Often, today, the chief emphasis in recitation and declamation is placed on prose content. But that is only a makeshift. The prose content of a poem, what lies in the words as such, is of little importance; what is important is the way the poet shapes and forms it. Ninety-nine percent of those who write verse are not artists. In a poem everything depends on the way the poet uses the musical element, rhythm, melody, the theme, the imaginative element, the evocation of sounds. Single words give the prose content. The crux is how we treat that prose content; whether, for instance, we choose a fast or slow rhythm. We express joyful anticipation by a fast rhythm. If we say: The hero was full of joyful anticipation, we have prose even if it occurs in a poem. It is essential, in such an instance, to choose a rapidly moving rhythm. When I say: The woman was deeply sad, I have prose, even in a poem. But when I choose a rhythm which flows in soft slow waves, I express sorrow. To repeat, everything depends on form, on rhythm. When I say, The hero struck a heavy blow, it is prose. But if the poet speaks in fuller, not ordinary tones, if he offers a fuller u-tone, a fuller o-tone, instead of a's and e's, he expresses his intention in the very formation of speech.

In declamation and recitation one has to learn to shape

language, to foster the elements of melody, rhythm, beat, not prose content. One has also to gauge the effect of a dull sound upon a preceding light sound, and a light sound upon the following dark one, thus expressing a soul esperience in the treatment of the speech sounds. Words are the medium of recitation and declamation: a little-understood art which we have striven to develop. Frau Dr. Steiner has given years to it. When we return to artistic feeling on a higher level we return to speech formation as contrasted with the modern emphasis on prose content. Nothing derogatory shall be said against prose content. Having achieved it through the naturalism which made us human, we must keep it. At the same time we must again become imbued with soul and spirit. Word-content can never express soul and spirit. The poet is justified in saying: "If the soul *speaks,* alas, it is no longer the soul that speaks." For prose is not the soul's language. It expresses itself in beat, rhythm, melodious theme, image, and the formation of speech sounds. The soul is present as long as the poem expresses rising and falling inner movements.

I make a distinction between declamation and recitation: two separate arts. Declamation has its home in the north; and is effective primarily through the weight of its syllables: chief stress, secondary stress. In contrast, the reciting artist has always lived in the south. In recitation man takes into account not the weight but the measure of the syllables: long syllable, short syllable. Greek reciters, presenting their texts concisely, experienced the hexameter and pentameter as mirrors of the relationship between breathing and blood circulation. There are approximately eighteen breaths and seventy-two pulse-beats per minute. Breath and pulse-beat chime together. The hexameter has three long syllables, the fourth is the caesura. One breath measures four pulse beats. This one-to-four relation appearing in the measure and scanning of the hexameter brings to expression the innermost nature of man, the secret of the relation of breath and blood circulation.

This reality cannot be perceived with our intellect; it is an instinctive, intuitive-artistic experience. And beautifully illustrated by the two versions of Goethe's *Iphigenie* when spoken one after the other. We have done that often and would have done so today if Frau Dr. Steiner were not indisposed. Before he went to Italy, Goethe wrote his *Iphigenie* as Nordic artist (to use Schiller's later word for him), in a form which can be presented only through the art of declamation, chief stress, secondary stress, when the life of the blood preponderates. In Italy he rewrote this work. It is not always noticed, but a fine artistic feeling can clearly distinguish the German from the Roman *Iphigenie.* Because Goethe introduced the recitative element into his Northern declamatory *Iphigenie,* this Italian, this Roman *Iphigenie* asks for an altered reading. If one reads both versions, one after the other, the marvelous difference between declamation and recitation becomes strikingly clear. Recitation was at home in Greece where breath measured the faster blood circulation. Declamation was at home in the North where man lived in his inmost nature. Blood is a quite special fluid because it contains the inmost human element. In it lives the human character. That is why the Northern poetic artist became a declamatory artist.

As long as Goethe knew only the North he was a declamatory artist and wrote the declamatory German *Iphigenie;* but transformed it when he had been softened to meter and measure through seeing the Italian Renaissance art which he felt to be Greek. I do not wish to spin theories, I wish to describe feelings which anthroposophists can kindle for the world of art. Only so shall we develop a true artistic feeling for everything.

One more point. How do we behave on a stage today? Standing in the background we ponder how we would walk down a street or through a drawing-room, then behave that way on the stage. It is all right if we introduce this personal element, but it does lead us away from real style in stage direction, which always means taking hold of the spirit. On the stage, with the audience sitting in front, we cannot behave naturalistically. Art appreciation is largely immersed in the unconsciousness of the instincts. It is one thing if with my left eye I see somebody walk by, passing, from his point of view, from right to left, while, from mine, from left to right. It is quite another thing if this happens in the opposite direction. Each time I have a different sensation; something different is imparted. We must re-learn the spiritual significance of directions, what it means when an actor walks from left to right, or from right to left, from back to front, or vice versa; must feel the impossibility of standing in the foreground when about to start a long speech. The actor should say the first words far back, then gradually advance, making a gesture toward the audience in front and addressing both the left and right. Every movement can be spiritually apprehended out of the general picture, and not merely as a naturalistic imitation of actions on the street or in the drawing-room. Unfortunately people no longer wish to make an artistic study of all this; they have become lazy. Materialism permits indolence. I have wondered why people who demand full naturalism—there are such—do not adopt a stage with four walls. No room has three. But with a four-wall set how many tickets would be sold?

Through such paradoxes we can call attention to the great desideratum: true art in contrast to mere imitation. Now that naturalism has followed the grand road from naturalistic stage productions to the films (neither philistine nor pedant in this regard, I know how to value something for which I do not care too much) we must find the way back to presentation of the spiritual, the genuine, the real; must re-find the divine-human element in art by re-finding the divine-spiritual.

Anthroposophy would take the path to the spirit in the plastic arts also. That was our intention in building the Goetheanum at Dornach, this work of art wrested from us. And we must do it in the new art of eurythmy. And in recitation and declamation. Today people do breathing exercises and manipulate their speech organism. But the right method is to bring order into the speech organism by listening to one's own rhythmically spoken sentence, which is to say, through exercises in breathing-while-speaking. These things need re-orientation. This cannot originate in theory, proclamations and propaganda; only in spiritual-practical insight into the facts of life, both material and spiritual.

Art, always a daughter of the divine, has become estranged from her parent. If it finds its way back to its origins and is again accepted by the divine, then it will become what it should within civilization, within world-wide culture: a boon for mankind.

I have given only sketchy indications of what Anthroposophy wishes to do for art, but they should make clear an immense desire to unfold the right element in every sphere. The need is not for theory—art is not theory. The need is for living, fully living, in the artistic quality while striving for understanding. Such an orientation leads beyond discussion to genuine appreciation and creation.

If art is to be fructified by a world-conception, this is the crux of the matter. Art has always taken its rise from a world-conception, from inner world-experience. If people say: Well, we couldn't understand the art forms of Dornach, we must reply: Can those who have never heard of Christianity understand Raphael's Sistine Madonna?

Anthroposophy would like to lead human culture over into honest spiritual world-experience.

www.ingramcontent.com/pod-product-compliance
Lightning Source LLC
LaVergne TN
LVHW051009080826
845145LV00009B/2533

* 9 7 8 0 8 8 0 1 0 1 5 4 7 *